The World According to Razor

My Closest Shaves

Neil Ruddock

with

James Hogg

CONSTABLE

CONSTABLE

First published in Great Britain in 2020 by Constable

1 3 5 7 9 10 8 6 4 2

Copyright © Neil Ruddock and James Hogg, 2020

The moral right of the authors has been asserted.

A CIP catalogue record for this book
is available from the British Library.

ISBN: 978-1-47213-531-5 (hardback)
ISBN: 978-1-47213-530-8 (trade paperback)

Typeset in Bembo by Hewer Text UK Ltd, Edinburgh
Printed and bound in Great Britain by Clays Ltd, Elcograf, S.p.A.

Papers used by Constable are from well-managed
forests and other responsible sources.

MIX
Paper from
responsible sources
FSC® C104740

Constable
An imprint of
Little, Brown Book Group
Carmelite House
50 Victoria Embankment
London EC4Y 0DZ

An Hachette UK Company
www.hachette.co.uk

www.littlebrown.co.uk

For Leah, who got me back on the straight and narrow
and made me the happiest man on earth.

Contents

Introduction

All right, dickhead? How's it going? Ready for a bit, are we? Want some, do ya? Yeah! YEAH! YEAH!

All right, all right, calm down.

Just a couple of words to the wise before we kick off, OK? First of all, some of the language in this book is a little bit fruity so if you're a sensitive soul who watches *Songs of Praise* and thinks that swearing belongs in the boozer then might I suggest you put this down now and go and knit yourself a scarf? The thing is, when I start telling a story Mr and Mrs F usually make an appearance, and when Mr and Mrs F make an appearance the B family usually turns up and then the Cs come storming in, God bless 'em. I was going to try and tone it all down a bit but then that wouldn't be me, would it? It would be Razor light, and last time I looked they were a fucking band. As with my days as a footballer, it's all or nothing with me, and you my son, or daughter, are getting the lot.

As it says on the cover, this book is the world according to my incredible self. That's my world, by the way, not the world in general. Once again, if you were expecting to read Razor's views on politics or the fucking EU then you're going to be disappointed. Anybody who wants to read that needs help! This is yours truly talking about some of the experiences that have helped to create the absolute fucking legend what is *moi*. You'll find the odd footballer in here, not surprisingly, not to mention the odd pop star and actor. There's even a world leader! Some of the tales involve a bit of mischief and most involve a drink or two. Most importantly of all, though, they're all a bit of a laugh so if I were you I'd get yourself a big drink, settle down somewhere quiet, turn off the notifications from Pornhub on your phone and have yourself a nice little read.

Right then, children, are we sitting comfortably?

Then I'll fucking well begin.

Regrets? I've Had a Few . . . Hundred!

Anyone who says they've never had any regrets in their life isn't telling the truth. The difference is how long you hang on to them. Personally, I try and let them go as quickly as possible and just move on. As importantly though, I always try and learn from them. I mean, what's the point in making a tit of yourself or making a pig's ear of something if you can't take something away from it?

I've had some fucking scrapes though. God, have I? I've also got away with murder in the past – metaphorically speaking – and one of the first regrets I ever had in football was an incident that, if my manager hadn't believed my excuse, could have finished my career before it had even begun. Subsequently, letting this particular regret go has been quite hard, which is why the story's worth retelling. Seriously, ladies and gents, if you want a blueprint for how not to behave at the very start of your career then have a word with me. I am that blueprint!

OK, picture this if you will. It's 1985, I'm sixteen years old and I've recently been signed as an apprentice by Millwall Football Club. Half my family supported Millwall when I was a kid and the other side supported Fulham, but with my two older – and bigger – brothers both supporting Millwall there was never any doubt as to which of the two teams would end up with my support.

Since getting into football it had always been my ambition to play for Lions of Millwall but as it turned out I was lucky to get spotted, let alone offered a contract. We were living down in Ashford at the time, which is sort of in the sticks so you had more chance of being kicked by a snake than you did being picked by a scout. Then, one day, a very good friend of mine called Mark Tworts suggested I go and play for his Sunday team, St Thomas More in south London, and a few months later I was picked up by Millwall. I actually owe Mark a lot as if I'd carried on playing for Ashford it's very doubtful I'd have progressed to be a professional. Anyway, at least we know who's to blame!

Incidentally, as a kid I always played up front and it wasn't until after I signed for Millwall that I became acquainted with defensive duties. We were playing a friendly down at Gravesend one day and were short of players at the back.

'How do you fancy playing centre half?' asked Theo Foley, who was George Graham's assistant.

Without thinking I said, 'Sure, I'll give it a go.' I'd never played there before but so what? I was obviously keen to impress and just wanted to play. George Graham used to like his boys playing out of position during training occasionally and I think it paid dividends. It certainly did for me.

I ended up putting in quite a good shift in that game, even if I do say so myself. I was good in the air and managed to snuff out their centre forward no trouble. So impressed were the management at my defensive debut that, apart from on a couple of occasions when I went back to the club a few years later, I never played centre forward again. Even so, in my final year as an apprentice I ended up scoring twenty-six goals and all from centre half! I must have been literally shitting talent.

Anyway, on to my regret. In March 1985 Millwall were drawn against Luton in the quarter final of the FA Cup and me and a few thousand other Lions fans made the journey up to Kenilworth Road to cheer on our team. I don't know exactly what started the trouble but it might have had something to do with us Millwall fans not being happy about having bricks thrown at us in the away end, but to be fair to the Luton fans it wasn't going to take much either way. The atmosphere before the match had been moody to say the least and both sets of fans had been waiting for an excuse to kick off. Not me, of course. I was sitting in the family stand on my own eating a hotdog and reading a copy of *Shoot*.

When the touch paper was finally lit all hell broke loose. Seats were ripped out and thrown on to the pitch, after which a battle began between the Millwall supporters and the police with the supporters using anything they could get their hands on as weapons. Advertising hoardings and seats being the most popular. By this time, I'd discarded my copy of *Shoot* and was on the pitch asking everyone to calm down. Honest! Then, when it all started getting a bit nasty, I decided to make myself scarce.

The following day on the front cover of the *South London Press* there was a large photo of the pitch battle between the Millwall fans and the police plastered right across the front page under the headline HOOLIGANS. And there, right in the middle of the photo asking everyone to calm down and stop being so nasty to each other, was me. Oh boy, was I in the shit. The feeling that went through me when I first saw my ugly mug was one of total fear. I was only too aware of how much trouble I was in and when George Graham called me in to see him the following day I feared the worst. George was a proper disciplinarian and he didn't take shit off anyone, least of all a first-year apprentice. My excuse that I was trying to get away from the trouble was actually true, to a point. I'd realised at some point during the action that my presence might get me into trouble and at the time the photo was taken I was genuinely trying to find the exit, m'lud. Fortunately for me George believed my story and he forgot about it.

I didn't. Had he not done so I'd have been out on my ear and with a reputation that would have made most managers think twice about signing me. I'd been very, very lucky and vowed that I would learn from my mistake and never do anything stupid like that again. If anyone can smell bullshit at this very moment in time I'm afraid it's probably me.

A few weeks later, me and the lad I shared digs with, Gary Middleton, went out for the night and we ended up in Pizza Hut in Pimlico. We weren't pissed or anything but we ended up having a bit of a handbags confrontation with another couple of lads and, instead of letting it die out like it would have done, the manager called the police. That's right, it was his fault!

By this time I'd acquitted myself well in both the youth team and the reserves and I'd been told by George that if I kept it up it wouldn't be long before I was knocking on the door of the first team. That's if I didn't fuck everything up, of course!

Fortunately, the police didn't charge us with anything but they did inform George what had happened. Having already been given the benefit of the doubt on one occasion I feared that my luck had run out and the hours in between George summoning us and actually seeing him were absolutely fucking torturous. Ever since the Kenilworth incident I'd been super aware of how George reacted when somebody pissed him off and he didn't mince his words. Nor did he just let people off without punishment.

By the time it came to us arriving at his office I'd convinced myself that I was on my way out. My parents were over in Saudi Arabia at the time as that's where Dad worked and I had visions of him being summoned back in order to deal with me. As big and brave as I thought I was, and I did, I was scared out of my fucking wits.

Our coach, Roger Cross, who would end up coaching me at West Ham many years later, the lucky bastard, and who had a hugely positive influence on my career, went into George's office before us to plead our case. When he came out again and told us to go in I couldn't read his face for love nor money. It was getting scary now.

As we walked in and closed the door behind us everything was quiet. George was standing behind his desk with his back to us and just for a split second I thought the benevolence he'd shown during our previous encounter might not have been a one-off. I was wrong. He went totally fucking bananas.

To echo George's words, we'd let ourselves down, we'd let our families down and, most importantly, we'd let the club down. The club that had shown so much faith in us and had given us a chance. When he then shouted the well-used phrase, 'I'm going to teach you boys a lesson you'll never forget,' I feared the worst. It got better though, as he followed it with the words, 'You're both on ground duty for the next two weeks. Now get out of my sight!'

Ground duty meant doing odd jobs around the stadium such as painting and cleaning. The fact that we were doing odd jobs at the stadium obviously meant that we were still apprentices at Millwall Football Club and that was all I cared about. Even so, I was absolutely gutted after that roasting from George and, regardless of what I may or may not have got up to later in my career, it did have an effect on me and I did alter my behaviour – which beggars the question, imagine what I'd have been like if he hadn't bollocked me?

Fucking hell!

One of my first regrets on the field of play took place during an England Under-19 tour of South America. This seventeen-day tour should have been one of the highlights of my career so far and if it hadn't been for two pieces of red cardboard being waved at me by a tiny tosspot dressed in black then it would have been. The previous year I'd been on a tour of China with the same squad and that had been amazing. The food was a bit iffy at times but some of the sights we saw were out of this world, not least the Great Wall of China. The only thing I didn't like about that were the stairs. There must have been about 3000 of them and because it gave us such a decent work-out we didn't have to train afterwards. The highlight football-ing-wise was playing China in the National Stadium in front of a hundred thousand people. The majority of the squad were playing for reserve sides at the time so we were used to playing in front of two or three thousand people. Walking out in front of a hundred thousand was unknown territory but instead of letting it intimidate us we rose to the occasion and won. I know I'm a biggish lad but I felt like a giant on that pitch. There can't have been one player for China who was over 5 foot 7. They were bloody fast though. We managed to get to the final of the tournament but were beaten 2–1 by Brazil. That was no disgrace though. They were a good side.

The highlight off the pitch on that trip was being taken to Hong Kong for three days. That place makes London look like a sleepy little village. It's mad! One of the first things I did when I got there was buy myself a load of dodgy Lacoste T-shirts and fake Rolex watches. When I got back home I took one of the watches into training with me.

'What's that?' asked one of my fellow apprentices, pointing at it.

'That's a Rolex,' I said proudly. 'It was a gift from the Chinese Ambassador. The whole squad got one. They're worth about six thousand pounds each.'

The lads had been well jealous about me going on the tour in the first place and when they heard about us playing in the National Stadium and getting through to the final – which I'd been kind enough to tell them about while we were over there – they were fuming. This, though, was the icing on the cake. 'You mean you got given a six-thousand-pound watch just for going on holiday?' one of them asked.

'That's correct,' I said triumphantly. I even went out and got a brochure for the watch from a top jeweller to corroborate my story. They never found out.

Anyway, where was I? That's right, I was in Brazil about to make a huge tit of myself.

One of the most exciting things about this trip – apart from how little the women appeared to be wearing – was the fact that Bobby Robson and his number two, Don Howe, were running the show, which gave us all an opportunity to show the men at the very top what we were capable of. Others in our squad included David Hirst, Michael Thomas, Kevin Pressmen, Matt Le Tissier, Paul Merson, Paul Ince and Vinny Samways, so there was no shortage of talent.

Before our first match Mr Robson paid us a visit in our dressing room and after wishing us all well he made it clear exactly what he expected of us. Plenty of endeavour and cool heads were his main two requirements, and he really went to town on discipline and behaviour. At the World Cup in Mexico the previous year Ray Wilkins had been sent off against Morocco for an incident that had been described as 'a disgrace', and it was clear that the manager didn't want any similar indiscretions from any of his young charges. As if!

During the first match against Brazil I went in for the kind of firm but fair tackle that are – or should I say were – meat and potatoes at home and I won the ball. What I should have done before making the tackle was consider the fact that the game is played differently in Latin American countries. Had I done so I might not have gone in so hard and the player I tackled might not have rolled around on the pitch fifteen times, called for his mother and a priest, and put on the kind of performance that would have earned him a leading role in a really shit daytime soap opera. On top of this, the referee was also Brazilian so I didn't stand a cat in hell's chance. Out came the card, and off went the defender. Bollocks!

Mr Robson was relatively sympathetic and as I was walking off the pitch he assured me that these sort of instances weren't uncommon. It was nice of him, but I felt like such a plank.

In the next game against Uruguay I got punched by one of their players. Not being the sort of person to let something like that go I squared up to the numpty straight away and thought about ripping his head off. Before I could level the score with him the referee jumped in so I barely made contact. Because of this, and because the ref had been standing right next to us when I was punched, I assumed he'd send the Uruguayan player off and perhaps give me a caution for reacting like I did, but he didn't. He sent us both off.

Before this tournament I had never been sent off before, at any level. In fact, I don't think I'd even been booked. I wasn't Gary Lineker, but in those days – in the UK at least – you had to either whack the referee, break somebody's nose or do a wanker sign to the club chaplain to get booked. Not like today. They give them out like Smarties these days.

Having never watched it back I can't really tell you what my reaction might have looked like to anyone watching but I can't see how it could have merited a red card. Anyway, the damage was already done and as much as I wanted to remonstrate with the ref and tell him what a wanker he was, I had to go. I didn't want to make it worse.

While we're on the subject of double embarrassments on a football field, I have had two happen during the same game before, and within seconds of each other. I still wince when I tell this story. It happened when I was playing for Liverpool and involves a certain player called Rui Costa, who at the time was playing for Fiorentina. During the match, which was away at Fiorentina, he nutmegged me, not once, but twice in succession. I hate this bloke!

He'd been winding me up for the whole of the first half so when we came out for the second half I thought, *Right then, you twat, I'm going to have you!* I really wanted to hurt him. About ten minutes in I saw my chance but as I flew in to do him he got the ball on the outside of his right foot and put it through my legs.

'Olé!' shouted sixty thousand Fiorentina supporters.

I thought, you absolute shithouse. I really am going to hurt you now.

I immediately turned around and before I could even register what was happening the bastard got the ball on his left foot and did the same thing again.

'Olé!' shouted the crowd. I'd had a bloody double!

The game ended up going to penalties and in addition to me scoring mine, Costa missed his and we ended up going through. It was obviously past the point where I could injure him physically (without getting arrested) so I ran straight up to him after we'd won and gave him about a hundred *olés*, right in his face. *Olé, you useless twat. Olé!*

But if being sent off against Brazil was a bit embarrassing – and I was – being sent off against Uruguay in the following game was devastating, and it wasn't even my fault. Honest guv!

What was actually missing from that story was a bit of the old red mist, which is something I became famous for back in the day, or should I say infamous. Sure, I may have lost my temper a bit with that Brazilian player, but that was just me playing football. The red mist is something that, over the years, got me into an awful lot of trouble and gained me a reputation as being, to quote one newspaper, 'Britain's Hardest Footballer'. Believe it or not, that was not the kind of title I wanted to be labelled with as a professional footballer, especially when I was trying to win a new contract, which I was when they printed it. It was the culmination of a six-month spell in my career that had more mist than Dartmoor on a wet February morning – just coloured red – and more anger than an episode of *EastEnders*.

The season in question, which was 1991–2 while I was at Southampton, had got off to an awful start after I was sent off for a professional foul on my old teammate Rodney Wallace, who'd just been sold to Leeds. Rod was clean through and apart from taking off a boot and trying to throw it at him I had no option but to bring him down, which I did. Because of the new ruling, that was now a straight red card and so I had to walk. After coming back after the suspension I started collecting yellows like Robbie Fowler collects houses and during November I was suspended for a few more games.

Now, instead of going home, taking stock and trying not to do it again, I persuaded myself that it wasn't my fault and by the time I came back – again – I was actually angrier than I had been prior to being suspended, if that were possible. Then, on 20 December 1991, during a game against Notts County, I lost the plot completely and afterwards my entire world caved in. It was all a bit ironic really because in the days leading up to that match I'd opened talks with my manager, Ian Branfoot, about signing a new contract. Despite the cards, I was in a really good place at the time. The family were all settled and happy and I was playing for a good club. The money wasn't fantastic but believe it or not that was never the main motivation with me. I was more interested in the pubs and the kebab shops! But because the family were happy I knew that my next contract, should it be forthcoming, was going to be an important one and the better my final season the better my chances were of being offered something decent. Anyway, it's time for me to walk the plank.

The incident itself took place about a minute before the final whistle. Notts County had just equalised and I'd gone from being quite calm and relaxed to wanting blood, and preferably Craig Short's. He'd been winding me up for most of the bloody match but because we'd been in the lead I'd managed to ignore it. Then, once they'd equalised, every move and gesture he made seemed like an insult directed straight at me. I was looking for an excuse to batter him, basically, and a couple of minutes later I found one. After a fracas with Alan Shearer, Craig Short seemed to stamp on him while he was down and without giving it a second thought I was off in his direction. He and Alan must have been about 50 or 60 yards away from me when it happened and after arriving at my destination I grabbed hold of Craig Short's collar, questioned his parentage and stuck one on him. Short needed to have four stitches after the match but surprisingly nothing was said, to me at least, until the following day. It was obviously just the calm before the storm.

When Ian Branfoot came to see me in the players' restaurant and informed me I was being fined and transfer-listed, I almost brought up my bloody lunch! Seriously, I felt sick to the pit of my stomach. I don't think I'd heard of a player being transferred because of an on-the-pitch incident before. 'The FA will undoubtedly have something to say about it,' were Ian's parting words to me, and after that I was made to train with the kids. The following day the papers were absolutely full of it and I can honestly say that it's the worst Christmas I've ever had. I'd been told after the incident, by Branfoot mainly, that the chances of another club coming in for me were minimal and without actually saying it he was indicating that, in his opinion, I may as well start looking for a job as a security guard which, incidentally, was the career path David Pleat once suggested I take during my spell at Spurs. More about him later.

After a few months playing with the youth team, by which time I was fitter than I'd ever been, thanks mainly to the youth coach, Ray Graydon, I was recalled back to the first team. Ray had also helped me sort out my head while I was with him and although I was still prone to making the occasional cock-up, thanks to him I was a lot better than I had been. The team went on a great run after my return – winning an impressive six games on the spin at one point – and after that the manager was all over me again. I have to say this came as somewhat of a surprise as in the weeks after the incident he'd gone to great lengths to make me feel virtually unemployable. It's funny how things change, don't you think?

Speaking of which, a few weeks later I was called into the chairman's office and after exchanging a few pleasantries – that hadn't happened in a while, I can tell you – I was offered a new contract, with double the fucking salary! They certainly hadn't been offering that before. So what had changed?

Despite all that, even an idiot like me knows when it's time to go and as far as me and Southampton were concerned, it was definitely time to go. Actually, that's a lie. I don't always know when it's time to go. If a landlord shouts, 'Time at the bar gentlemen please,' and I'm having a giggle, I'll sidle over and ask for a lock-in. Sure, I was still having a giggle at Southampton, but too much water had passed under the bridge and I think I needed a change.

So, what's the moral of this particular story? Let me have a think. Oh yes, I know. Don't headbutt people. It's wrong!

One thing you can't do if you've been involved in as many incidents as I have is bear a grudge. All it does is eat you up and, just like regrets, it's best to let them go. One person who seems to have a problem with this is the great Stuart Pearce. I did him once while I was playing for Southampton and he's never forgotten it. He used to smash it to Nigel Clough for a one-two and on this occasion I read it and I ended up two-footing him. His reaction was ever so slightly over the top and from then on, whenever we played against each other, he'd always make a point of having a go. It gets worse, though, as when we played together at West Ham he would deliberately go on the opposite team to me in training just so he could do me. It's now thirty years since the original tackle took place and he still won't let it go. Whenever I see him he comes straight up, ribs me and says, 'Remember that tackle, Razor?'

'Stuart son,' I say, 'it was thirty years ago and you're nearly sixty. Let it go, son, let it go!'

The other one I have to mention here is Andy Cole, who blocked me on Twitter a while ago when I tried to apologise for breaking both his legs. Although I'm having a laugh with this, one thing I'm not doing is trying to glorify violence on the football field and the first thing I should say before I tell you the whole story is that throughout my career I never once set out to injure a player on the ball. I may have wanted to hurt one or two of them, but I only set out to injure people when I went for them off the ball. OK? I'm glad that's cleared up.

The incident in question actually happened during a reserve game while I was playing for Liverpool and him Man United. I'd met Andy a few times before that on England B duty and although we'd always got on I'd found him a bit arrogant. A typical striker, basically. Like myself, he was on his way back from injury at the time and despite it being the reserves the match was played with all the passion and commitment you'd expect from a game between Liverpool and Man United. The incident, which took place at Anfield a week before our respective first teams were due to meet, was a straightforward fifty–fifty affair which I was determined to win, just as I was every challenge. Unfortunately, I ended up landing on Andy. It was only the following day that I learned the extent of his injuries. I hadn't even been yellow-carded for the tackle and had won the ball so as far as I was concerned my conscience was clear.

Even so, I was genuinely upset about what had happened and went to great lengths to try and apologise to Andy and see how he was. Understandably perhaps, neither he nor the club chose to return my calls so I tried to leave messages instead. The press had an absolute field day with it as it fitted perfectly with my reputation and, as far as they were concerned, made an absolutely blinding story. With nobody interested in telling my side it was obviously seen, at least by the fans who read the papers, as being a straightforward assault. Death threats from the United fans came in thick and fast. I used to get bullets through the post with Razor written on the side of them, which the police used to take away to analyse. Saying that, I also used to get thank-you letters from Newcastle fans!

After that, whenever I played at Old Trafford I wasn't allowed to warm up as I used to have darts thrown at me. Getting off the coach could also be a bit tasty and it was like running the gauntlet. The first time I played there after the incident I deliberately put a load of cotton wool in each ear before the match so it was dangling down to my shoulders. Not to block out the sound, but to wind the United fans up. I just couldn't help myself! Anyway, as we were standing in the tunnel before the match waiting to go on, a policeman came up to me, took out the cotton wool and slapped me across the head. 'You'll cause a riot you fucking dickhead,' he said.

'Sorry boss,' I said.

I'm my own worse fucking enemy sometimes. Apparently the atmosphere was quite hostile during the game but it's often hard to tell at Old Trafford. Atmosphere, what atmosphere? See, I knew I'd get my chance.

Over the years I have tried to make contact with Andy – sorry, Andrew, as he's now known – and have apologised publicly dozens of times, but he always gives me the fob off. This, I have to admit, probably has as much to do with me as it does him because over the years, while being interviewed, I have played up to it once or twice and have even said things like, 'I used to love kicking Andy Cole.' I also said something along the lines of, 'I only meant to break one of his legs. I must have sat on the other one!' Everyone suffers from a bit of foot-in-mouth disease occasionally. I just happen to be riddled with it!

2

God Once Shat in My Shoe

Tuesday 12 September, 1995, is a date that will stay with me for the rest of my born days. I was in Russia with the Liverpool team playing FC Spartak Vladikavkaz in the first round of the UEFA Cup, although that's not the reason the date is etched on my brain. We went on to win the game 2–1 in front of about forty-five thousand people, but again, that's not the reason. Because I'm a bit forgetful, something pretty remarkable has to happen in order for me to remember a date and, as per the chapter title, they don't come more remarkable than God taking a dump in your fucking shoe. Or at least they don't where I come from. You might be different. What makes this even more extraordinary is the fact that I invented this particular God. Confused? You fucking will be.

It all happened on the plane home. After the match, as you'd imagine, we all got involved with a few beers and what have you. Now, whenever I have a kip on a plane I always take my shoes off first, or in this case my Reebok Classics (other trainers are available). You remember the ones that Status Quo used to wear that had the Velcro at the top? Fucking mint they were. Anyway, I was wearing a pair of those with no socks and about halfway through the flight I felt like having a kip. So, after downing my beer I took them off, sat back, and closed my eyes.

I must have woken up about an hour later and one of the first things I noticed was I had a semi on. I don't know about you but having a kip at altitude usually results in me getting a little visit from Woody Allen. It's the closest I've ever been to the Mile High Club and at my age I'm just grateful it still happens. When I woke up on this particular occasion I was also busting for a piss and with the rest of my body still waking up I felt around on the floor with my left foot for the corresponding Reebok. Having located it, I slipped in my foot and repeated the process with my right foot. This one was a little bit more difficult to find but after locating it I pushed the tongue back with my toes and got my foot into position. By this time, my bladder was about the size of a fucking melon so I pushed my foot into the trainer as fast as I could and started undoing my seatbelt. Unfortunately, the time it took me to notice that there was something inside my trainer was longer than the time it had taken me to get my foot completely inside. The moment it registered, I knew exactly what it was. Somebody had taken a fucking poo in my shoe.

My instinct to go ballistic and start tearing up seats was defeated by the fact that I'm not overly keen on the smell of shit, especially other people's. Instead, I carefully pulled my foot out of the trainer, had a quick look (why do people do that?) and hopped off to the bogs.

Back in 1995 I was quite a bit lighter than I am now. Even so, I was still six-foot-two and quite heavily built so how the hell I was going to clean shit off my foot in a little cubicle I had no idea. It's hard enough taking a piss inside one of those aeroplane lavs for someone my size so this was definitely going to be interesting. The shit had gone in between my toes and even under my nails. It was fucking rank!

After managing to close the bog door behind me, which in itself was an achievement, I attempted to get my foot in the direction of the sink. The thing is, the further north my foot went the stronger the smell became and so every time I tried getting my foot inside the sink I started to retch. After about four tries I managed to get it in there without puking up and after pulling out a handful of bog roll I turned on the tap and started cleaning off the shit. I've had to do some pretty difficult things in my time but trying to scrape somebody else's shit from under my toenails in an aeroplane toilet on a flight back from Russia at about one o'clock in the morning is up there with the best of 'em. Or should I say worst?

It took me about ten or fifteen minutes but after a lot of hard graft I was finally satisfied that my right foot was a shit-free zone. After returning to my seat I picked up the soiled trainer, handed it to one of the hostesses and asked her to dispose of it. Once that was done, it was on to finding the culprit and, once I'd located him, punishing the cunt good and proper. Somebody was going to die for this, there was no question. It was time to address my colleagues.

'Right then, you bunch of cunts,' I said, leaning over the back of my seat. 'Which one of you thought it would be a good idea to take a dump in one of my Reebok Classics?' As you'd expect, the majority of the suspects were pretending to be asleep with a small minority remaining awake and trying not to laugh. I figured that anyone daft enough to stay awake and giggle at me wasn't going to be the culprit so one of them would have to become my grass. The question was, who? I eventually decided upon Trigger (Robbie Jones) and after beckoning him to join me in the galley I prepared to state my terms.

'Right then,' I said, 'tell me who shat in my Reebok Classic or I'll fucking kill ya.'

The direct approach seemed to have an effect.

'It was Robbie Fowler,' said Trigger immediately.

'Really? I was the one who christened that bastard God, for fuck's sake!' I could not fucking believe it. 'All right Trig,' I said, 'piss off back to your seat.'

Actually, I could believe it. Robbie's undoubted mercurial talent was matched only by his genius for rubbing people up the wrong way, especially me. He was the cheekiest of cheeky little bastards that one, and he had a mouth on him like the Mersey Tunnel. Somebody with that amount of talent is always going to be a little bit cocky and despite what he did in my shoe he was the best all-round goal scorer I ever played with, and that's including Clive Allen who, during the 1986–7 season, scored forty-nine goals in all competitions playing up front on his own.

Anyway, now that I knew who the culprit was I had to decide what to do with him. My initial idea – it was more like a long-ing really – was to get the offending trainer and then march up to his seat and push it into his face before pulling him into the gangway and giving him a hammering but having to smell that little wanker's shit again put me right off. And the fact that there was a fair chance it would piss off the captain of the plane, not to mention the gaffer. Nope, I was just going to have to bide my time on this one.

We landed sometime in the middle of the night and while the rest of our party were a bit sleepy after getting off the plane I was like a fucking hawk. There was only one thing I wanted – Fowler's blood – and what's more I was going to have a drop. I decided to let God believe that he might have got away with it by leaving my retaliation for as long as possible so I waited until we'd been through passport control and had collected the luggage. Once we'd done that, I was ready.

After picking up my bag from the carousel I saw where he was, walked straight over to him and – BOSH! I gave him one from the shoulder right on the fucking chin. There was bumfluff everywhere. It didn't quite knock him out but it took him an eight count to get up again.

'What did you do that for?' he said while getting to his feet.

'You pooed in my fucking shoe, you cunt!'

'Oh yeah,' he said. 'Fair enough.'

With that I picked up my stuff and hobbled out of the airport wearing my one remaining Reebok Classic. What a way to make a living!

3

Ossie, Ossie, Ossie

People don't believe me when I tell them that as a child I used to be quite quiet. The thing is, when you've got two older brothers like I have who were never backward in coming forward, you don't get that many opportunities to talk. I was also a bit shy, which again people tend to think is a load of bollocks. 'Razor Ruddock, shy? Fuck off!' It's true though. One thing I did do when I was a kid was listen to people I respected, so despite eventually turning into a gobshite my ears were always flapping and I'd soak up pieces of advice like a sponge does water.

Apart from 'Give your arse a break and your mouth a chance, you fat cunt,' one of the best pieces of advice I've ever been given came from one of the true legends of the game, Osvaldo César Ardiles. When I signed for Spurs from Millwall in 1986 I was his bitch. Seriously! I used to make him cups of tea. Back then all the senior players were assigned a junior player each who would clean their boots and what have you, in return for them being given the benefit of their experience. It was almost like an apprenticeship scheme and luckily for me I was assigned to Ossie. I said luckily because he took the initiative seriously so in addition to me training and playing with the great man, which was obviously a pleasure and a privilege – not to mention rooming with him which was less of a pleasure and a privilege – I was also party to some occasional words of wisdom. Granted, I couldn't understand most of them on account of him sounding like Speedy fucking Gonzales but the ones I caught made perfect sense.

That was the culture at Spurs in those days. Everybody mixed. If the senior players and their wives or girlfriends were going up west to see a show or were going for a meal or something we'd get invited too, as would our girlfriends. I'm pretty sure it was a deliberate move by the club and it made life better for everyone both on and off the pitch. We younger players were a bit star struck and at the end of the day it's a lot easier to go out and play with your friends than it is people you're in awe of.

The piece of advice I'm referring to was uttered by the great man shortly before my first game for the club which, due to the fact that I never made it into the first team at Millwall – at least for a league game – was also my league debut as a professional footballer. No pressure then! We were at home against Charlton and I don't mind admitting that I was absolutely bricking it.

About ten minutes before we were due to leave the dressing room Ossie came over and sat next to me. He obviously knew I was nervous. In fact, I'm pretty sure I was biting my nails at the time.

'Son,' said Ossie after sitting down, 'this is your first game for Tott-ing-ham, yes?'

'That's right, Ossie,' I replied.

'You look very nervous,' he said. 'OK, let me give you some advice that will help you and make you feel better. When Ray Clemence passes you the ball and you cannot pass it to either me or Glenn Hoddle and you are being closed down by the striker, do you know what to do?'

The picture he was painting was doing nothing for my nerves but I decided to go along with it. 'No,' I said, expecting him to say something inspiring or insightful. 'What should I do?'

'Fucking panic!' said Ossie. Then the little sod started laughing, which set me off. I'll tell you what, that was exactly what I needed, a bit of a giggle, and we went on to win the game 1–0. What a lovely, lovely man, and what a player! If only he could speak English more proper, though, like what I do.

One of the most astute things Ossie Ardiles ever said to me was, 'Razor, no wonder you're a fat pisshead hooligan. When you're at Tottenham we get sponsored by Holsten, when you're at Liverpool you get sponsored by fucking Carlsberg and when you go to West Ham you get sponsored by Doc Martens. It all makes perfect sense!' Joking aside, he did have a point. Beer, beer and bovver boots. Get in, my son!

Speaking of which . . .

The hardest thing I've ever had to explain to anyone in my entire life is when me and Ossie went to watch a girls' football match. We were playing Brighton away in the FA Cup and across the road from our hotel was a football pitch.

'What's going on, Razor?' asked Ossie.

'What do you mean?'

'The people playing football are girls,' he said.

'What's wrong with that? Ain't you ever seen a girls' football match before?'

'No,' he said. 'Never.'

'Fancy having a look?'

We ended up going to watch this match for a few minutes and when one of the players scored a goal her dad, who was on the touchline shouted, 'Get in there, my daughter my son!'

Ossie said, 'Did I just hear that right? Why did he call his daughter his son?'

I thought, here we fucking go. Go forward twenty minutes and the match has finished but I'm still standing there trying to explain to Ossie why the dad had called his daughter my son. Some things just do not translate I'm afraid, and out of sheer desperation I ended up buying him a few drinks.

It was actually Ossie Ardiles who taught me how to play golf. We all had memberships at Crews Hill Golf Club in London when I was at Spurs and because I was Ossie's bitch he used to take me down there a lot. Ossie loves his golf and he's been playing for donkey's years. He still plays off eighteen though, the cheat. He was a good teacher and I've been playing regularly ever since. I even got my handicap down to three at one point, which is probably close to what Ossie's should be. He always nicks my fags too, the little shit.

A mate of mine bought a golf club about half a mile away from me in Ashford. It's called Kingsnorth Golf Club and I'm a life member. I go there all the time and I treat the place like it's my own. I just walk behind the bar and help myself. My mate who owns it always goes, "Ere, what you doing?' and I always say, 'You'd do the same to me.'

'Oh yeah,' he says. 'I would!'

Ossie and me did a dinner a couple of years ago in London. England had just been beaten by Croatia in the semi-final of the World Cup so to be honest I wasn't really in the mood for it. Ossie was, though, and with the prospect of having to spend the evening with a depressed England fan staring him in the face he set about trying to get us both pissed. Funnily enough he succeeded and after doing our stint – we were interviewed before and after the dinner – we carried on drinking.

Ossie might be able to pull the wool over his golf handicap on occasion but when it comes to how much he's had to drink there's no hiding place. And when Ossie Ardiles has had a drink you know he's had a drink. Four times I tried to get him into a cab and each time he'd turn up about five minutes later and order another drink. On the fifth attempt I decided to stay with him until the taxi driver had driven off and just before closing the door he told me to stop. He was absolutely hammered by this point, bless him. He then started unbuttoning his shirt and I thought, *Oh my God. He's going to strip off!* Fortunately, he only undid two buttons and after reaching inside his shirt he pulled out his World Cup winners' medal, which he'd obviously been wearing all night without telling anybody, waggled in the air, blew me a big theatrical kiss and said, 'Drive on.' I just stood there for about ten minutes pissing myself laughing.

On 1 May 1986 Ossie had his testimonial at White Hart Lane and the spawny little git managed to get Maradona along. We were playing Inter Milan and when the little genius arrived at the stadium he didn't have any boots. I'm pretty sure he ended up borrowing a pair of Clive Allen's and wore one of Glenn Hoddle's shirts. Thank God it was before the Hand of God incident in Mexico as I'm not sure the reception he received from the thirty-thousand-strong crowd would have been quite as enthusiastic. In fact, I think we'd have lynched the little fucker! I certainly would.

As I was new to the club I was only a sub but at least it meant I got to go in the dressing room and warm up with him. Before the match somebody chucked him a ball and he suddenly started tapping out a rhythm with it using his foot. It's one of the most bizarre things I've ever seen but you know how basketball players can bounce a ball very quickly quite low to the ground and do loads of tricks, Harlem Globetrotter bollocks? Well, Maradona was doing that with the bottom of his foot and he was tapping out some sort of rhythm. A tune, almost. He was chatting away to Ossie at the same time and the rest of us just sat there with our chins on the floor.

When we went out to warm up he started doing some proper tricks. The one I remember most clearly was him booting the ball up in the air and then making a circle in front of him with his arms. A few seconds later the ball went through the circle without touching the sides and he caught the ball on his foot. It was unbelievable! At the end of the game I managed to blag a big signed picture of him and a couple of weeks later I asked my mum where it was.

'Oh, I gave it to the paper boy,' she said.

'Whaaaaaaaaat?'

'Well, I didn't think you wanted it. Did you want it? Oh, sorry love.'

4

Heroes

We've all met people who walk on a different plane to ourselves. I'm not just talking about famous people or even talented people. I'm taking about special people. People who make a genuine difference to the world.

The first person who fits into this bracket for me personally is the aftershave king from Doncaster, Mr Kevin Keegan. Kevin was like a clean-cut version of George Best. Mums adored him and wanted him to marry their daughters, dads admired him and wanted their sons to play like him, teenage girls drooled over him and boys like me just idolised him. You didn't have to be a Liverpool supporter or even a football supporter to love Kevin. He was the complete package. The first kit I had bought for me as a school kid was a Liverpool strip. Not because I supported them. I was Millwall through and through. It was all because of curly-haired Kevin. That was the impact he had on me and millions like me, although I did stop short of buying that piss he used to advertise with Henry Cooper. What was it, Brut? I wasn't going to be splashing that all over, thank you very much. It fucking hummed. Some people will do anything for money (cough cough).

Incidentally, when I was ten or eleven I even had a Kevin Keegan perm. Try imagining that. It's not easy. Then, when he ended up going to Hamburg I went off him a bit and started modelling myself on people like Glenn Hoddle and Ian Botham. It was fucking mullet time!

Since becoming a professional footballer (before turning into an absolute fucking legend) I've been lucky enough to meet Kevin on quite a few occasions and I'm proud to say that he's ended up becoming a friend. Some people say that you should never meet your heroes and I admit that the first time I met him I was a little bit nervous. *What if he's a wanker?* I asked myself. *He looks like a wanker. A proper wanker.* Fortunately for me, Kevin's everyman quality, which is something he's become famous for over the years – almost as famous as he is for saying 'I'd love that' – is as genuine as his love for the game of football and you couldn't wish to meet a nicer bloke. He probably is a bit of a wanker though. Aren't we all?

A few years ago at Christmas time a well-known book-maker from Ireland with the initials P. P. invited me and few other old pros over to Dublin for a drink or ten in a boozer. They called it 'Pundits in a Pub Talking Shite', which was catchy – and accurate – and they also did one for rugby union and horse racing. There was me, Jason McAteer, Wes Brown and Mr Keegan, with some geezer holding court. It was a right laugh. How lucky am I though, eh? I got paid good money to sit around a table in a boozer in Dublin with two mates and one of my all-time heroes having a few pints and a chat. Bingo!

Off the pitch, the most impressive human being I've ever had the pleasure of meeting, apart from Phil 'The Power' Taylor, is Nelson Mandela, or Deller, as we used to call him on the pub darts team. He was shit, by the way.

We ended up meeting Nelse, which is what we actually ended up calling him, on Liverpool's end-of-season tour to South Africa. When Roy Evans, the gaffer, first suggested it nobody was quite sure what to say really. It was still a bit dangerous over there and after an awkward silence one of us – I forget who – said as much. 'Oh, don't worry about that,' said the gaffer. 'We've been on to the Embassy and everything. It'll be fine! We'll be going to Johannesburg first and then on to Cape Town. It'll be great!'

As it turned out Liverpool and Aston Villa had both been invited to go and play in a tournament over there, which was billed as an International Soccer Festival. As well as us it would also feature Kaizer Chiefs, Cape Town Spurs and Manning Rangers, and would last about ten days, including a long weekend at the end when we'd be able to do some sightseeing. Not a bad way to make a living, even if things were a little bit tasty over there.

The closest I came to getting into serious trouble was when we played Cape Town Spurs at Newlands Cricket Ground. I'd never played football on a cricket pitch before – not a professional one – and it was all a bit weird. Before the match, the groundsman had asked us to avoid the wickets if we possibly could but at the time I wasn't listening and I only learned this afterwards. The weather was absolutely appalling that day – it had been raining since the day before – and after scoring a particularly brilliant goal which was my second of the match I did a full-length Klinsmann right up the main wicket. I basically dug a trench down it! At half time the groundsman went ballistic and had he been a bit younger and a bit bigger I think he might have had a go at me. My size fortunately saved me on that occasion, unlike his wicket! Apparently wickets take years to prepare so I actually did feel for him a bit and tried several times to apologise. Oh well, I was never much of a cricket fan.

We set off to South Africa on the Saturday morning and were flying from Manchester to Heathrow and then from Heathrow to Johannesburg. Because it was end of season we were straight on it the moment we arrived at Manchester and even by the time we got to Heathrow we were already quite merry. Well, I definitely was. After arriving at Heathrow we had to collect our luggage and check in again for some reason and when the woman at the check-in desk asked me if I had anything in my bags I decided to have a joke with her. She looked like she was game for a laugh so I thought I'd give it a go. 'Just a couple of Uzis,' I quipped. 'Oh yes, and about thirty hand grenades.' At that moment, the woman I thought was game for a laugh quickly reached under her desk and hit a button, and as she did I had a feeling that my joke might not have been taken as such. And I was right. First of all a siren started that wouldn't have sounded out of place during the Blitz and as well as lights flashing everywhere a very loud voice came over the Tannoy. 'EVACUATE TERMINAL NOW. EVACUATE TERMINAL NOW. DO NOT TAKE YOUR LUGGAGE. EVACUATE TERMINAL NOW. EMERGENCY, EMERGENCY.'

Despite knowing full well that this was all on account of me I turned on my heels and had it away with the rest of the passengers, but after only getting about fifty feet I was surrounded by ten armed police officers and told to get on my knees and put my hands behind my head. A few seconds later I'd been handcuffed and was lying on my front being frisked. When they eventually pulled me to my feet I couldn't believe what I saw.

A few minutes ago there'd been about four thousand people all about to go on holiday and now all that was left was their luggage, which was scattered all over the place. It was then that the enormity of what I'd done and what was happening started to hit home. The ten armed police officers had already given me a good idea but seeing the terminal like that was just weird.

'I was only having a laugh,' I started saying instinctively. 'I promise. I'm not a terrorist. I'm a footballer! Seriously lads, I'm really sorry.'

As I carried on pleading the armed police carted me off and put me in an interrogation room where I was left for about an hour and a half. In that time they obviously must have corroborated my story with the gaffer and checked my luggage for Uzis and hand grenades. Apparently that alone took over half an hour because they had to get the bomb squad to do it with specialised equipment. Fuck me, was I in trouble!

As all that was being done I was told to strip off, and once I'd done it, somebody wearing gloves did a very thorough search of my personage. Very thorough! The only thing they didn't do was put a finger you know where, and no matter how many times I asked them they wouldn't do it. Once that was done I had to go through a metal detector naked and after that I was allowed to get dressed.

After being shown back to the interrogation room I waited a while and then a couple of anti-terror police officers came in and started interrogating me. Well, they'd come to the right place, I suppose. My only line of defence was that I'd been a bit pissed at the time and was only having a laugh. Despite being true, this was treated with disdain by the officers and they went out of their way to make me realise what an idiot I'd been. To be fair, they didn't have to try that hard. I knew full well! Once they'd finished with me the gaffer then arrived and apparently he'd also been read the riot act by the anti-terror police for not controlling his players. I could tell he was fuming. After doing some more apologising and assuring the police that I would never do it again I was released with the gaffer back into the community.

'Gaffer, I'm really sorry,' I said once we'd left. 'I promise you it was just a joke. If I'd had any idea what was going to—' Before I could complete my grovelling apology the gaffer decided to pass sentence and let me know the punishment.

'You're not having another drink until we get to South Africa,' he said.

'WHAAAAT?' I cried. 'But that's about twelve hours.'

'I know,' he said smiling.

As it turned out Roy Evans had needed to plead with the police not to charge me which, given the seriousness of the offence, joking or not, would probably have thrown the entire trip into jeopardy. It would have been squeaky-bum time apparently and the fact that I escaped with just a twelve-hour drinking ban – as difficult as it was – probably wasn't too bad. He must have done some fucking arse licking though, old Roy. Apparently the chief of police there still has a season ticket at Liverpool. JOKE! How he did it, though, I have no idea, because the list of things they were going to charge me with was massive. All the flights had to be delayed, you see, and situations like that obviously cause chaos and cost lots and lots of money. Had it been today I'd never have got away with it. God no.

While we were on the plane I did everything I could to try and sneak a cheeky vodka in here and there but the gaffer had told everybody about the ban – the players, the coaches, the physio, the cabin crew, the captain! The world and his bloody wife seemed to know that I wasn't allowed a drink. Honestly, I'd rather have stayed at home!

I have to hold my hands up and say that when we met Nelse I didn't know that much about him. I knew about apartheid and the fact that he'd fought against it, and I also knew that after being released from prison he'd become the leader of South Africa. Despite that, this bloke definitely had an aura about him and when we were introduced I remember being a bit taken aback. It's hard to put your finger on it but when Nelson Mandela walked into a room it was as if he brought everyone together. Does that sound a bit flowery? Coming from me, it probably does. Do you know what though? I couldn't give a monkey's. He was a bit special.

Unsurprisingly, it did kick off while we were over there, but it was all over in a flash. It happened at the stadium in Johannesburg. We had a match against Kaizer Chiefs and before the match Nelse walked into the dressing room with a couple of bodyguards in tow. The thing is, nobody told us he was coming so one minute we were sitting there taking the piss out of each other waiting to go out and play, and the next minute we were in the presence of one of the most famous and respected people on the planet.

'Pleased to meet you, Nelse,' I said after being introduced.

He had a good handshake on him, I'll give him that. Then, before the game, we all lined up on the pitch and were introduced to him a second time.

'You again?' I said, shaking his hand.

Anyway, after the game had finished there was a knock on the dressing room and who was standing there but old Nelse.

'Bugger me, Nelse,' I said. 'You're like water you are, you get everywhere!'

Shortly after that Nelse was having a chat with Roy Evans when one of the lads shouted, ''Ere, gaffer, do you want a beer?' Unfortunately one of Nelse's bodyguards thought he'd said a different word, which I'd rather not repeat in this book and for a few minutes it all got a bit nasty.

'No, no,' said one of us trying to calm things down. 'He said gaffer! It's what we call the manager. It means boss!'

Fortunately, the bodyguard accepted our explanation and everything calmed down very quickly. It could have gone either way though. After that, we all got changed and went out on the piss, with Nelse and his bodyguards! How many people can say they've been out on the piss with Nelson Mandela? Not many. I don't think he got a round in though. Typical bloody world leader. Tight as a duck's arse.

5

Cry Me a Razor, or Big Men Do Cry

As the title suggests, even big hairy lugs like me can shed a tear from time to time. Not all the bloody time. I'm not Gazza or John Terry or Thierry Henry or Cristiano Ronaldo or David Seaman or Jack Wilshire or Neymar or Pelé or Gianluigi Buffon or Mario Balotelli, all of whom have cried like little children on the field of play. Oh no. When I shed a tear it's because the world has basically come to a fucking end. Either that or because I've been watching *Little House on the Prairie*. Cuts me up every time.

The last time I really cried – this was tears of anger *and* upset, so double bubble – was when Roy Evans dropped me for the 1996 FA Cup final which took place on 11 May 1996 and was against Liverpool's old enemy, Man Utd. The 1995–6 season had started off well for me. I'd been called into the England squad for a friendly against Colombia and despite not getting a sniff of the action (sorry) I was playing and feeling well. Then, in November, I went and did the splits at Middlesbrough – accidentally – and I was out for six weeks. After a quiet Christmas with absolutely no alcohol or fattening food whatsoever I got back into training and ended up making my comeback against Leeds in the league. We twatted them 5–0 that day and I scored twice so it was welcome back Razor. Two games later I was on the treatment table again and as well as being on the sidelines I was also in the doldrums.

Having to get fit and then remain fit, injury after injury, is bad enough but the problem I had at Liverpool was that every time I got injured somebody would step up, impress the gaffer by playing well – how bloody dare they? – and have the audacity (another big word there) to keep me on the bench. It was a complete fucking outrage from start to finish and I'd never been as frustrated. Or angry. I was always bloody angry! Had it been a similar season to either one of my first two at Liverpool I'd have been a first-team regular and would also have been a contender for the European Championship squad. As it was, I'd have been lucky to get into the reserve team the way things were going.

Fortunately, the last two months of the season improved and as well as playing the final five league games I also played in the quarter-final and semi-final of the FA Cup, both of which we won. Because of this I was beginning to feel like my old self again and I got it into my head that I would be a shoo-in for the final. Razor Ruddock was Wembley-bound and even the gaffer, Roy Evans, had indicated that he was going to stick with the same team that had started the last few games.

The Friday before the final was my birthday and with my first ever Wembley appearance now just a few days away, not to mention a possible winner's medal, I was in good spirits. In fact, I was the life and soul of the training field. The only thing that was different that day, apart from it being my birthday, was that the gaffer was very quiet. I kept trying to gee him up and have a laugh but for some reason he wasn't interested. He wouldn't even make eye contact with me. Then, as I was running past him chasing a ball, he stopped me.

'I need to talk to you, Raze,' he said.

I'm normally quite good at picking things up but I promise you I had absolutely no idea what was coming. If anything, I thought he was going to tell me he was ill or something. That's how confident I was of being in the squad for the final.

'What is it, gaffer?' I said. 'Is everything OK?'

'No, not really, Raze,' he said. Again, he failed to make eye contact. 'Look. I don't know how to tell you this but you haven't made the final.'

'What do you mean?' I said. It still hadn't clicked.

'I mean you haven't made the team for the final. You're not going, Raze.'

Now it clicked. For once in my life I was speechless. Properly speechless. I just stood there looking at him in disbelief.

'I'm sorry,' said the gaffer.

'Sorry?' I said finally. 'It's my fucking birthday!'

That obviously had fuck all to do with the situation but I was just starting to feel a tiny bit sorry for myself and at the time it felt relevant. I brought the meeting to a close by telling the gaffer to fuck off, after which I went back the dressing room and balled my bloody eyes out. I think it was shock as much as anything. Had I been expecting to get dumped I could have readied myself for the drop but I wasn't. I was already on my way up the fucking tunnel!

The initial shock was gradually replaced by the realisation that my chance to fulfil a childhood dream had now gone and, realistically, with regards to the FA Cup at least, was unlikely to happen again. As a consequence, instead of the tears dying down a bit after the initial shock had subsided, they kept on coming, and as everything started to sink in the sadness turned to anger and then back to sadness again. I was a bleeding mess, to be honest.

After getting changed I took myself off for a couple of beers. The idea, obviously, was to console myself but that was an impossible task. I'm not one for feeling sorry for myself but I don't think I've ever felt as gutted or let down in my entire life. It's every English player's dream to play in the FA Cup final and when your opponents are Manchester United and you play for Liverpool it gives it that edge. In fact, from my own point of view and in my current situation, it didn't get any better. Not now though. I wasn't even going to be on the fucking bench! The gaffer had decided to bring Phil Babb back into the team and play him alongside John Scales and Mark Wright, so that was me out. I had nothing against Babbsy. Me and him were best mates back then and deep, deep down I was actually happy for him. Honest! It was the way it had been handled by the gaffer that pissed me off, not to mention the fact that I thought my recent performances had at least merited a place on the bench. Two days before though, and on my fucking birthday!

'Ere, Razor, what did you get for your birthday? Aftershave? Socks?'

'No mate, I got denied a game at Wembley.'

And the Oscar for Best Performance by a Fat Whingeing Git goes to . . . me!

I can whinge all I like but at the end of the day the gaffer's the one who picks the team and he's obviously the one responsible. What I had to understand was that his decision wasn't personal and I admit that I often had problems making that distinction. Once again, it was my reputation that got in the way, as whenever a decision or a situation went against me I'd immediately think, *That's because it's me, isn't it?* Paranoid? Me? When this happened I thought the whole world was against me. For a while at least. Reputations follow you around like shadows and if I could have my time again I'd go to much greater lengths to learn how to deal with that and separate my real self from my public persona and my persona in the game.

When the papers got hold of it Roy said it was like having to tell a sixteen-year-old apprentice that he isn't going to make it and that the club's letting him go. I suppose that made me feel slightly less angry towards Roy, but not for long. At the end of the day I was going to be missing what should have been the biggest game of my career and if anything his comments made it worse. It was the worst possible end to the worst season of my career so far and I took no pleasure in the fact that the lads lost the game to an Eric Cantona goal. Anyone but him, for fuck's sake! Worse still the goal was a bit sloppy and had I been in my rightful position I would no doubt have tidied things up, raced up the other end, turned Eric's collar down, kissed him on both cheeks and then put the ball through Schmeichel's legs and into the back of the net. See what you missed, boys!

6

Best of the Best

It'd be hard for me not to do a quick chapter on the best footballers I've played with and against. Let's keep it to three of
each, though, or we'll be here all bloody day. The three best
footballers I ever played against were Eric Cantona, Dennis
Bergkamp and Gianfranco Zola. There are others I could
mention such as Emilio Butragueño, Jean-Pierre Papin and
Salvatore Schillaci, but that was in Europe so the games were
just a one-off. You see, when I played there was no Champions
League or anything. Only the winners from each country went
through to the European Cup and the UEFA Cup was still a big
deal. They had some proper fucking teams in it back then. In
fact, when I played against Papin and Schillaci, who were playing for Bayern Munich and Inter Milan respectively, it was in
the UEFA Cup.

These days you haven't heard of half the teams that compete
in what is now the Europa Cup and quite a few of them aren't
even full time. The Europeans always had the best shirts,
though, I'll give them that. I've got quite a collection at home
and I've got some decent domestic ones too. One of the most
valuable I ever owned was Eric Cantona's 1996 FA Cup final
shirt in which he scored an eighty-fifth-minute winner against
my club, Liverpool. Yes, that's right. I had a shirt from a final

I wasn't even picked as a sub for. Just to remind myself of the pain.

After I'd split up with my first wife, my boy Josh, who's now 30, rang me up and asked me if he could borrow eight grand.

'What the hell do you want eight grand for?' I asked him.

'I want to go to Vegas with the boys,' he replied.

'You fucking what? With eight grand!'

The divorce had not gone in my favour – surprise, surprise – and to be honest I didn't have that kind of money. At least not to give away for a beano to Vegas. Just then, I had an idea. 'I'll tell you what,' I said to him. 'Don't tell your mum but go upstairs, get the Eric Cantona shirt and bring it round. There's a football memorabilia sale coming up at Sotheby's. Let's whack it in and see what happens.'

What will tickle you most about this story is how I came to own Cantona's shirt in the first place. I'm obviously going off on a tangent a bit here but you'll just have to bear with me. Eric, Dennis and Gianfranco aren't going anywhere.

After the match had finished and Man United had won the FA Cup, I wandered into the dressing room and sat down next to where Johnny Barnes was getting changed. The lads were obviously all still very down and I was pretty down too. Anyway, as I'm sitting there I suddenly see Eric Cantona's shirt sticking out of the top of John Barnes's bag. Fuck me, I thought. I'm having that! Across the dressing room I saw another Man United shirt, except this one had been chucked on a bench. *I wonder whose that is*, I thought to myself, and then I stood up and walked towards it. After turning it over I saw it had the name 'May' on the back. David May! Fucking get in there. After making sure nobody was looking I picked up the shirt, wandered back to

John's bag and swapped Eric Cantona's shirt for David May's. I then made myself scarce and hid the loot somewhere safe. A fair swap? Well, it was from where I was sitting.

After taking the shirt to Sotheby's I had to sign a contract that said I was the one who'd swapped shirts with Eric. Well, I'd swapped shirts with John, who'd swapped shirts with Eric, so it was near enough. A few days before the sale, Sotheby's got in touch with me and said that Man United had been on the phone to say that they had Eric's shirt in the Man United museum.

'That's bollocks,' I said. 'I'll tell you what, get them to send you a photo of it,' which they did.

When the photo arrived the shirt they claimed was Eric's FA Cup final shirt had short sleeves. The players were always given one of each but everybody knows that Eric Cantona only ever wore the long-sleeved version. When I put this to Man United they had to admit that they were mistaken and so the shirt went into the sale. It ended up selling for a whopping £15,000. I got seven and my boy got his eight. Happy days.

A few years ago me, John Barnes and Jan Mølby did a theatre tour of the UK and I ended up telling this story live on stage. The thing is, at the time of me telling it I still hadn't told John what I'd done so it came as a bit of a surprise. He almost fell off his chair! 'I bloody knew I had Cantona's shirt,' he said, giving me a whack on the arm. Poor John. He'd have been lucky to get £15 for David May's.

I have been on the receiving end of this, by the way, but on a slightly smaller scale. When we played against Inter Milan in the UEFA Cup once I managed to get Schillaci's shirt and a few days after the match I received a telephone call from the father of a good pal of mine.

''Ello Razor, it's Harry here. Jamie tells me you got Schillaci's shirt the other night. Look son, I'm opening an Italian restaurant in Bournemouth next week. Will you lend me it?'

'Yeah, course I will, Harry,' I said. 'No bother.' So I sent him the shirt.

About four years later I was watching an Inter Milan match when I suddenly remembered about the shirt. *Fucking hell*, I thought. *I'm going to have to get that back!* I phoned up Harry and said, 'H, any chance of getting my Schillaci shirt back? It's been a while!'

He said, 'Nah, I sold that restaurant. Don't you worry about it, son.'

'I'm not worried,' I said. 'I just want it back!'

'Nah,' he said. 'Shirt went with it,' and then he hung up.

OK, let's get back to the subject matter. One of the many things that separates geniuses like Cantona, Bergkamp and Zola from mere mortals like myself is the fact that they didn't have to think too much about what they were doing. They had that much natural talent that when a ball was passed to them they had no idea what they were going to do with it. It just happened. That was one of the first things that occurred to me when I started playing against players of that stature and to be honest I found it terrifying. I used to think to myself, *What chance do I have if I have no idea what they're going to do?* At the end of the day, though, you have to play to your strengths and one of mine was recognising that each one of these players had a weakness. Which brings me on again to my mate Eric.

When he kicked that mouthy little Crystal Palace fan in the chest during the 1994–5 season it's fair to say that everybody involved in the game, from fan to footballer, was shocked to the core. Nothing like that had ever happened in the professional game before and it gave me an idea. Eric might not have had to think too much about what he did with a ball but there was obviously still a lot going on in his head, and if I could get inside there for a bit and cause a bit of a trouble . . . well, who knows? I wanted to wind him up, basically, and put him off his game. Without him beating me up, preferably. It was going to be a very fine line though.

The idea for how to go about this came from a comedian friend of mine called Willie Miller. It was actually a dare and if there's one thing I find hard to resist other than a pint, it's a dare. 'I dare you to play with his collar,' said Willie.

'Done,' I said immediately. I didn't need asking twice. We were playing United the following week and luckily for Willie and his dare, I was marking Eric.

The first time I did it I just started playing with it. There was no need to go mad on the first date. I was bloody nervous though. Eric's about an inch taller than I am and he's obviously quite volatile. And hard! It's that fine line I was referring to. I wanted to wind him up to the point of his mind not being on the game, rather than his boot being on my nuts!

On the second attempt, I decided to turn his collar down, which is when I got my first bite.

'Fook off,' he said, putting it back up.

Gotcha, I thought.

I didn't say a word and continued as if nothing had happened. I then did exactly the same thing again, and then again and then again. On the fourth occasion, he swung an elbow at me and it just missed my face. This was working like a dream! About ten minutes later I had yet another go and this time he snapped, launching into a knee-high tackle from behind that got him a yellow card. Had it been today it would have been a straight red but that was never my aim with this. All I wanted to do was put him off a bit, and only because I admired him so much as a player. It was actually the ultimate compliment, although I doubt Eric would have seen it that way.

After turning down his collar for probably the twentieth time he turned around, looked me straight in the eyes and said, 'Me and you, we fight in ze tunnel.'

What, the Channel Tunnel?

Joking aside, Eric had the look of a madman when he said this and I was slightly taken aback. It was his turn to put me off!

As we played out the final few minutes of the game I wondered what the hell was going to happen. If I got into a full-on scrap with Eric in the tunnel we'd both be in big trouble and neither of us could really afford that. It might seem like cowardice to some but having started all this it was up to me to stop it going any further so, with that in mind, I walked straight up to David James, who is as big as a house, and asked him to walk off with me. Yes, I know what you're thinking. What a fanny! As I said though, I was trying to save me and the mad Gaul from starting our own Waterloo. Scared? Of course I bloody was! I'm brave, but I'm not stupid. If you'd seen his eyes you'd have been the same.

I don't know what happened but when me and my body-guard walked into the tunnel Eric was nowhere to be seen so the fight had been postponed, for now. After getting changed I went straight to the players' lounge. Not because I was running away from Eric. I was desperate for a beer! That was one of the great things about that Liverpool team. Win lose or draw, we'd always have a drink with the opposition afterwards. In fact, it became something of a post-match ritual with us and we even had a saying, 'Win, draw or lose, first to the bar for the booze!' Sheer bloody poetry.

By the time I was halfway through my second pint I'd almost forgotten about my hoo-hah with Cantona. Then, all of a sudden, I felt a tap on my shoulder. *Oh shit*, I thought. I knew it was him even without turning around. When I did turn around, sure enough, there was Eric standing right in front of me. Just like him when he gets the ball, I had absolutely no fucking idea what I was going to say or do. The difference being that Eric's natural talent used to kick in and he'd ended up doing something spectacular. The only spectacular thing I thought about doing was shitting my pants, which would have been interesting. Instead, I just stood there looking like a dead sheep. Just then, Eric handed me a pint of lager before giving me a little wink and then, without saying a word, he walked off. Le fucking chicken!

Playing either with or against world-class players can be demoralising sometimes, especially when you know that you'll never be able to play at that level. For me personally, this experience arguably made my career and had it not happened I'm not sure I'd have turned professional. It was while I was captaining England Under-19s and over the course of my captaincy I got to play against the likes of Ian Rush, Tony Cottee and Graeme Sharp. At first they made me feel like I wasn't good enough to play the game, which was demoralising. They were so bloody good! In the end it actually inspired me to kick on as a player, which I did, so the experience did me a massive favour. Had it not happened I would have plodded on and may have missed that opportunity to kick on and improve. Once you get to twenty-two or twenty-three, I don't think you can kick on that much, so it was perfect timing.

Let's get on to Zola. Well, what can I say? The man was infuriating! He used to get into my head just by being a genius, so it's not that different to the experience I had with the Rushes, Sharps and Cottees. Rather ironically, I would retaliate in exactly the same way that Eric retaliated against me, in that I'd lash out and try and hurt him. Unfortunately, that was the only way I could handle a player of that quality, with drastic action! It was a mixture of fury and desperation really. I was furious because he was running rings round me and desperate because I knew he was going to score. He was a centre back's worst nightmare.

I'll tell you the mark of the man though. When I was playing for West Ham my son George was mad about Zola and asked me if I could get one of his shirts. The next time we played Chelsea I went up to Zola before the match and asked him.

'Of course,' he said.

The match, which we won, was hard fought and I kicked Gianfranco all over the park. When the final whistle went he ran straight off to the dressing room and I thought, *Oh well. I'll have to buy one!* It was fair enough though. He really had taken a hammering – pardon the pun. Anyway, about half an hour after the match Zola walked into the home dressing room with his shirt.

'Here you go,' he said. 'Would you like me to sign it for anybody?'

God, I was impressed. I even apologised for giving him a hard time, which made him laugh. What a professional though. He couldn't have been nicer!

Dennis Bergkamp was about the same size as me, which used to baffle and amaze me. I used to think, *How can somebody that big be so incredibly skilful?* What's the word? An enigma, that's it. Dennis Bergkamp was an enigma. Even so, Dennis did have a weakness and his was similar to Eric's, in that it was possible to affect him mentally. The reason I say similar and not the same is because with Dennis it was about confidence as opposed to anger. The only time I saw this first hand was when I was play-ing for West Ham, again. The game was obviously against Arsenal and shortly after kick-off, while waiting for a corner, Wrighty came up to me, pointed at Dennis who wasn't far away, and said in a really stupid voice, 'Razor, it's Dennis Bergkamp!' He then gave me a wink as if to say, go on, your turn.

''Ere, Johnnie,' I said to John Hartson in a stupid voice. 'Look, it's Dennis Bergkamp!'

Johnny looked at Dennis and said, 'Ooooh. He's GOOD, inne, that Dennis Bergkamp.'

After that, as the game went on, we stayed in character and kept going up to Dennis and telling him how GOOD he was. 'You're GOOD, you are!' 'Can I have your shirt after the game?' I said. 'No, I want it,' said Wrighty. 'Fuck off, he's giving it to me,' said Johnnie. 'I'll tell you what though, he's GOOD, that Dennis Bergkamp.' 'Oh, yeah. He's well GOOD. Inne, Wrighty? That Dennis Bergkamp?' 'What? Bergkamp? He's the best!'

Throughout the game we got Steve Lomas, Johnnie Moncur, Rio Ferdinand and Frank Lampard involved and Dennis was left in no doubt whatsoever that we thought he was – GOOD! We'd give it a rest for a few minutes and then one of us would shout, 'LOOOOOOK! IT'S DENNIS BERGKAMP! HE'S – GOOD!' And then it would all start again.

I have no idea if this had been Wrighty's intention or not but Dennis just couldn't get started in the game and he was taken off after about an hour. We'd obviously got into his head. If it was Wrighty's intention, it must have been based on something he saw at Arsenal. Either that or he was just taking the piss, as per usual. Actually, I think that'll be it.

While we're on the subject of getting into someone's head, when I was at Liverpool and I was playing against a young centre forward I'd always try and intimidate them at the start of the game. Robbie Fowler would usually start things off by saying in their earshot, 'Fuck me, Razor's lost it. He's going to hurt somebody today. Shit a brick!'

I'd then play along by grabbing hold of Robbie and going, 'Fuck off, you little cunt, or I'm going to hurt you!'

You could then see the young centre forward going, *Oh, for fuck's sake! I'm dead!*

After that I'd get hold of the centre forward and go, 'Look, sorry mate but I've got the right hump today. I'll tell you what, though, you win the first header, I'll win the second header, and I won't do you from behind, yeah? That OK with you? I'll tell you what, though, you run me into the corners and I'll break your fucking legs, OK?'

I did this to Alan Smith from Leeds once. I went through the whole speech having got hold of Robbie Fowler and after I'd finished he just said, 'Fuck off, you fat cunt!'

I said, 'You what?' I must have done that twenty times without hearing a peep from any of them when all of a sudden this little northern nutter tells me to fuck off and calls me a cunt!

'You're not meant to say that,' I said.

'I'm not scared of you,' said Smithy. 'Fuck off, you fat cunt!'

The little shit ran me ragged during the game and I was so impressed I ended up getting his shirt after the game. I said, 'Give us that here, you little shit.' He was only about seventeen years old at the time. Typical bloody Leeds player.

Although he wasn't on the original list I would like to give an honourable mention to David Beckham. I used to idolise that man. In fact, he was probably the only youngster I ever truly revered when I was playing football. Everyone else would have been either my age or senior to me.

Becks used to get so much fucking stick from the other fans it was unreal. I remember Man United coming to West Ham once. It was probably his first domestic game after being sent off for England and because the West Ham fans are usually very pro-England, the abuse he received was unbelievable. They chucked bottles and rocks at the Man Utd coach as it pulled in to Upton Park and every time he touched the ball they went crazy. His missus was in the crowd and she was also pregnant but she came in for just as much. I genuinely felt sorry for both of them, and to be honest I found the whole thing quite embarrassing. Ironically, David Beckham was one of the few England players from his generation who could block out all that bollocks and still perform for his country, and it certainly didn't affect his performances for Man United. That match finished 0–0, by the way, and the main talking point occurred after just three minutes when somebody looking suspiciously like me appeared to handle the ball in his own area. Fortunately, the referee turned down United's appeals for a penalty so I was able to breathe a massive sigh of relief!

The reason I liked David Beckham initially was because he reminded me of Glenn Hoddle. I think a lot of people my age will tell you the same thing and because of the amount of TV coverage that was now available – and the fact that he was playing for Man Utd, who had more coverage than anyone else – you could marvel at the boy whenever you liked.

As opposed to going through Beckham's career and picking highlights, which has probably been done a million times before, I want to tell you about something he did for a mate of mine called Aaron who is sadly no longer with us. Aaron used to manage an Under-15s team and when David was training with Tottenham in the winter of 2011, prior to going to America, Aaron asked me to ask Harry Redknapp if he could bring the kids up to watch Beckham and the team train. 'Course he can,' said Harry. I was going with Aaron and the youth team so Harry gave us the run of the place. When we sat down to watch Beckham train I was dumbfounded. He could do things with a ball that I didn't think were possible and each and every one of us just sat there open-mouthed.

Once they'd finished training, as opposed to disappearing like everyone else, Becks spotted the young lads and came over. He actually introduced himself to them, and nobody had asked him. He was there for about an hour in the end and he answered every single question and signed every single bit of kit and memorabilia. He even took the lads on the training pitch for ten minutes and did some kicking practice with them. I thought, *I fucking love you even more now!*

About two months after that I was in a pub in Camden with my brothers and some of their mates when all of a sudden I felt a tap on my shoulder. As you'll know by now, this usually spells bad news for me but when I nervously looked around, there standing in front of me was Becks.

'I'm sorry to interrupt you, Mr Ruddock, I can see you're with your friends. I just wanted to say hello.' After that he shook everyone's hand and left.

How can I possibly love this man any more than I do? I thought to myself. I don't know the boy very well at all so the only reason he did that was to give my friends a thrill and make me look good, and boy did that work! I didn't have to buy another drink all day.

I've heard a lot of people say that the more talented or famous people are the nicer they tend to be, and when it comes to Becks that's definitely the case. It's also probably why I'm such a cunt!

When it comes to choosing the best players I played along-side, that's a bit more difficult. The first player who made a real impression on me was Teddy Sheringham. I played with him at Millwall in the mid-1980s and at the time I was playing as a centre forward. He was just in a world of his own and is still the most intelligent and mature twenty-year-old footballer I've ever seen.

Going on to join Spurs and playing alongside the likes of Hoddle and Ardiles was obviously mind-blowing for me, but I was almost too in awe of them to appreciate who I was playing with. I also only made nine first-team appearances in that spell so I had other things on my mind. By the time I arrived at Southampton in 1989 I was a little bit more aware and could appreciate the talent that was around me more. Take Matt Le Tissier, for example. He was even slower than me yet he could make people look stupid with his skill. I've never seen another player be able to do that with the same ease and effectiveness as Matt, and it was incredible to watch. Baffling, but incredible. Then you had Shearer, of course, but at the time we didn't know how good he was going to be. The player who had the biggest influence on me at Southampton was without doubt Jimmy Case. He pops up all over this book and for that very reason. He was a five-foot-nine footballing giant, basically.

The one player who I wish I'd played alongside but didn't is Des Walker. He's a good friend of mine now and as a defender there weren't many I admired more. Had we played together I would have attacked everything and Des would have swept up. Each of us says that we would have been the perfect partner for each other and I still imagine us playing together occasionally. Loves a vodka and orange does Des. No ice. Lovely bloke.

7

The Great British Public

Because of who I am I tend to get heckled quite a bit when I'm doing talks. It's the hardman image coupled with the fact that I like a laugh. People think they can take the piss and to a certain extent they can. Like anything, though, there's a line which I'd rather you didn't cross. The trouble is, at the kind of events I talk at, alcohol is often consumed, and the more people drink the braver they become.

As with most speakers and comedians, I have an arsenal of putdowns that I can use on such occasions, some of which I've nicked and some I've made up. One of my all-time favourites is something I say when somebody shouts over me. That happens all the time when you're doing events and the sooner you embarrass a heckler the better as it prevents others giving it a go. One of my best putdowns is, 'Save yer breath, you cunt. You've got to blow your bird up when you get in.' Another one I like is, 'I don't talk when you're working, do I you dickhead? I just pick up my Big Mac and fuck off.' Those two always have the desired effect and after that people tend to just listen. And laugh, hopefully.

If an event becomes very boozy you'll often get dickheads shouting out random insults. This tends to happen if I go on late as the audience have had more to drink and, again, I've got a special bank of putdowns just for them. The last time it happened some bloke started shouting out 'Razor, you cunt,' every couple of minutes. Nobody laughed the first time so by the fourth time it was getting on everyone's tits. After spotting him I stopped the story I was telling and asked him to stand up.

'What's his name?' I said to one of his mates.

'John,' he replied.

'Right then, John,' I said, 'I've got a joke especially for you but you have to stand up before I tell it.' I could tell he was rattled but I wasn't going to let it go. 'Come on, John,' I said again. 'Get to your feet, son.' By this time, the rest of the audience had joined in and so John had no choice but to stand up. 'Right then, John,' I said when he was on his feet. 'This is a joke from me to you. There was an Englishman, an Irishman and a Scotsman, and they all thought you were a cunt. Right, you can sit down now, John.'

It wasn't so much the joke more the situation that had the audience falling about. Ninety-nine percent of people in an audience want to sit down, listen and be entertained, and if somebody becomes intent on spoiling that they need shutting up.

There's only one thing worse than a table full of pissed-up rowdy blokes at one of these events and that's a table full of pissed-up rowdy women! Honestly, blokes are nothing compared to birds when it comes to this and they're a lot harder to deal with. You can't just tell them to shut the fuck up and if you ever try and humiliate them you could be in big trouble. That almost happened to me in Wigan once. I was being heckled by a table of women and one of them got up to go to the lav. Quick as a flash I said, "'Ere love. There's only two things come out of Wigan: beautiful women and great rugby players. What position do you play?' The whole place just erupted and fortunately that included the rest of her table. She didn't half give me a look, though. I thought, you've dodged one there, Razor.

There's a fantastic comedian I work with sometimes called Jimmy Bright. He's got some absolute crackers when it comes to handling birds. My favourite is one he only uses in Wales. If there are a couple of women in the audience he'll always say, 'What part of Scotland are you girls from?' and they'll say, 'Wales, dickhead.' And he'll say, 'Sorry, what part of Scotland are you whales from?' It loses a bit on the page but if you hear it live in front of a good audience it's fucking amazing. Another comedian I work with, called Gary Marshall, is a Gooner hailing from Barnsley, bless him. Thank fuck he's got a sense of humour! He once said, 'I went to the zoo the other day and I saw two monkeys wanking. I then went to the lions and I was *still* wanking!'

OK, last one before we move on.

A wife calls her husband over. 'Here,' she says. 'You're a right cunt. Not only do I think you're a cunt but the next-door neighbours think you're a cunt, everyone in the street thinks you're a cunt, everyone you work with thinks you're a cunt, all our relatives think you're a cunt, everyone we ever meet thinks you're a cunt and if they ever had a competition to find out who's the biggest cunt, you would come second.' 'But why would I come second?' asks the husband. 'Because you're a cunt!'

OK, so what about on the pitch?

Well, for the first few years I never used to react very well to hecklers and sometimes I'd take it personally. That was until Graeme Souness started managing me. After taking a hammering from some away supporters one day I had a whinge at him. 'Fucking hell, boss,' I said. 'They gave me dog's abuse out there.'

'Yes!' he said, patting me on the back. 'And that's exactly what you want, son. That means you've got under their skin. Good lad! It takes the pressure off the strikers.'

I certainly wasn't expecting to be congratulated but fuck me, he was right. From then on I used to relish getting abused by the away fans and would take the piss out of them at every possible juncture. Some of it was good hearted, and the fact that it allowed the other players to play made it all worthwhile.

At the end of the day, though, I used to love a bit of banter and still do. Leeds and Sheffield Wednesday had some of the most vocal supporters and as soon as they started mouthing off I'd walk up to them, draw the shape of a house in the air and then mouth to them, 'That's my house that is. It's fucking massive!' Then I'd draw the shape of a tiny house and mouth, 'That's your house!' After that I'd do cars. I'd hold four fingers up and go, 'I've got four cars. Four! I've also got a Ferrari. That's worth more than all your Ford Focuses put together, you northern cunts!'

'Fuck off, Razor, yer soft southern bastard!'

'Yeah, up yours!'

Nine times out of ten you'd give them a thumbs up at the end of the game and get a standing ovation. I suppose it was banter, although it wasn't always that friendly. It's part of a

defender's duties, though, providing you have the right character. Make yourself the centre of attention with the opposition's
fans as soon as you possibly can. That's my advice.

One of the best heckles I ever heard was at Millwall, but it
wasn't from the away end, it was from the home fans. I was just
an apprentice at the time and there was one player there called
Dave Martin who, for whatever reason, used to rub the home
fans up the wrong way. I forget who we were playing but after
passing it about for about two or three minutes a fan shouted,
'For fuck's sake, Millwall, someone shoot!' and another geezer
went, 'Yeah, someone shoot Dave Martin!' Poor old Dave. He
didn't half get some stick.

When I was at West Ham one of the home supporters
shouted, 'Oi, Ruddock! Take that grand piano off your back!'
Not a piano. A grand piano! I'd have told him to fuck off if I
wasn't laughing so much. It was an absolute blinder!

One of the most famous hecklers of all was the bloke at West
Ham who used to sit behind Harry Redknapp and give him
stick constantly. 'You're fucking rubbish, Redknapp,' he used
to shout. 'Play four-four-two like West Ham did when they
won the World Cup, you cunt.'

As opposed to just ignoring him Harry would give him
some back. 'Drop dead, you fat twat!' I'd be sitting there pissing myself. 'Fucking shut up, Razor,' he'd say, 'or I'll drop
yer!'

This was home and away, by the way, so Harry would get it
week in week out. During a pre-season friendly at Oxford one
evening this bloke starts up as per usual. 'Are you still here,
Redknapp?' he said. 'Play four-four-two, you cunt! And why
are you playing Chapman? He's shit!'

We're all going, 'Can you hear him, Harry, can you hear him?'

'Yes I fucking can hear him!'

At half time Harry loses it completely and as we're walking off he goes up into the stands, grabs this bloke and drags him into the tunnel. We're all sitting in the dressing room with towels over our heads listening and Harry's going for him big time. 'I've had enough of you, you stupid fat cunt,' etc. Two minutes later the door opens and Harry's standing there with this geezer. 'Razor,' he said, 'this is the bloke you think's so funny.'

'I never said that, Harry!'

'Yes you did,' said Wrighty. 'You're always saying it.'

'Fuck off you!'

While me and Wrighty are arguing Harry drags this bloke, who's about forty, by the way, and about twenty stone, into the dressing room. 'Right then you,' he says. 'You're going to be West Ham sub for the second half.'

'I am not,' says this bloke.

'Yes you fucking are! You've been telling me for years how shit I am. Well, you can certainly talk the talk, mate, so let's see if you can walk the walk!'

We managed to get this bloke some kit and a pair of Rio Ferdinand's boots. He was size thirteen and this bloke was size nine. You should have seen the state of him. The thing is, Harry was still in a proper fucking mood so while we were all pissing ourselves laughing he was getting even angrier. 'Don't fucking laugh, you lot, this isn't funny!' Eventually Harry started cracking a smile or two and by the time we went out for the second half he was pissing himself like the rest of us. He wasn't going to let this bloke go though. No way!

As we walked back on there was an announcement over the Tannoy. 'There is an addition to the West Ham bench this evening,' said the announcer. 'Wearing number twenty-six, from Canvey Island, it's John Smith!' The fans all knew this bloke by name and when they heard him being announced they just erupted. As if it couldn't get any better, Harry then made him go and warm up on the touchline.

'Go on, you fat sod,' he said. The reception this bloke got from the fans was just incredible. 'Touch your fucking toes, you,' shouted Harry. 'Come on, get those knees up!' He was sweating like a pig, the poor sod, and there were people in the crowd laughing so much they were on the point of being sick. It was chaos!

With about five minutes to go Paolo Di Canio had to come off with a minor injury which meant only one thing. 'Oi, fatso,' shouted Harry. 'Get your tracksuit top off and get on that fucking pitch. Go on, go and be Trevor Brooking for five minutes.'

Instead of actually running and involving himself in the game, which I think would have been impossible, we just plonked this bloke on the edge of Oxford's box and told him to stay put. Then, on about the ninety-fourth minute, Johnny Hartson went past the keeper and was clean through on goal but instead of kicking it in he put his foot on the ball and called for John from Canvey Island. 'Quick, John,' he said. 'Come and boot it in. Come on!'

Harry's going, 'Nooooooo! Don't be a twat!'

It was too late though. As John from Canvey Island got within a couple of yards of his fellow striker, Johnny took his foot off the ball and John belted it into the back of the net. 'GOOOOOOOOOOOOOOOOOOOOOOOOOOOOAL!'

If somebody had told me earlier that day that Harry's heckling nemesis would end up replacing Paolo Di Canio and scoring a goal I'd have sent them to the bloody Priory. Amazing!

8

It's Funny Up North

In addition to football, having a drink and collecting vintage pornography, something that's always fascinated me is the origin of popular sayings. I don't know why that is. Certain things just interest me and the reason I'm including it in this book is because it might teach you ignorant morons a thing or two, so pay attention.

Take the expression, 'daylight robbery', for instance. Do you know where that comes from? Well, years ago you used to have to pay a tax on windows and if you didn't pay they used to brick them up, hence the term, 'That's daylight fucking robbery that is! Put those fucking windows back.'

Northerners have got some funny ones. I mean, where the hell does, 'I'll go to the foot of our stairs,' come from? The only explanation I could find on the internet was that the foot of the stairs was often the entrance to the cellar, which was the darkest and dankest place in the house. What difference does that make? It's always dark and dank up north! Speaking of which . . .

A few years ago I was doing a talk up in Huddersfield. I do quite a lot of talks in that area and they nearly always end up with a lock-in at wherever I'm staying. Funny that. On this occasion, I was staying in a pub just outside the city and at about two o'clock in the morning I wanted to get some fags. ''Ere, Bill,' I shouted to the landlord, 'I need to get some change for some fags. Can I get some from the till?' Now, if there were awards given for Yorkshireness, Bill's mantelpiece would be covered in 'em. Subsequently, I usually can't understand a fucking word he's saying so every time I ask him something I always do a bit of sign language, just to make sure. That's Razor sign language, by the way, not the stuff you see in the corner of your television screens. On this occasion I made a square to represent a till and then pretended to take coins out of it. I'm not saying that Bill's simple or anything but with somebody that northern you have to take precautions.

'Tin, tin, tin,' he said, and then buggered off down the cellar.

Fucking hell, I thought, *here we go. Rin Tin Tin? That was a bloody dog, wasn't it?*

When he emerged again a couple of minutes later I tried again. I could have got up off my fat arse, I suppose, but it was two in the morning.

'Bill,' I yelled, 'change for the fag machine, mate.' I didn't bother trying to make signs or anything. I just waved with both hands.

He wasn't happy.

'TIN, TIN, TIN!' he said again.

'Jesus Christ,' I said. 'I need a fucking interpreter in this place!'

In the end I got up off my fat arse, walked over to the bar and asked Bill very nicely if he'd mind repeating what he just said very, very, very slowly.

'Bluddy 'ell, Rayzer lad,' said Bill. 'Read maaaa bluddy lips. T'int – in't – tin.'

I was almost there so instead of asking him to repeat himself again, which would have finished us both off, I took a few seconds and tried to work it out.

'I've got it!' I said eventually. 'You said, "It isn't in the tin," which means you don't have any change!'

'By George,' said Bill. 'I think he's got it!'

'Does that mean I can't have any change then?' I asked him.

'No yer fuckin' can't. Naa get thee sen ter bed!'

But as much as I enjoy take the piss out of northerners, and Scousers, and Brummies, and Mancs, and Taffs, and Jocks, and Paddies, and those funny-sounding folk you get in the West Country who have hairy feet and say 'Ooh Aaaah' a lot, I love the different accents. In fact, I flatter myself that I'm something of a cunning linguist when it comes to impersonating different accents and can get my tongue around most of them, so to speak. Take Scouse, for instance. When I moved up to Liverpool all those years ago I was told that in order to understand Scousers you had to be able to speak like one, so that's what I did. I spoke like one whenever I could. The first things I was told to recite to improve my Scouse were, 'Tony Curtis', 'cheque book' (that's a B with an ooooh in the middle and then a K), 'yeah', 'Fuck off dickhead' and finally, 'Al 'ave an 'ooch', or 'I'll have a Hooch' in English. They were the staple names and phrases you had to use in order to learn Scouse, and probably still are.

What used to frustrate me about living up there was if you went to St Helens, which is only ten miles away, everything would change and you'd be back to square one again. 'What? Could you repeat that, love?' Where I live in Kent you can drive for a hundred miles and everyone sounds the same whereas up north it's like a different language. Geordies? No fucking idea mate. When a Geordie's talking to me I just nod occasionally and say, 'Yeah mate, absolutely.' It seems to work. Actually, I might try and learn Geordie one day.

One of the scariest places to go and do a talk is Glasgow, although the language barrier does prevent me from understanding some of the names they call me. Just like understanding Scouse, there are one or two things you can do up there that will make your life a lot easier. For instance, one of the first times I went up there to do a talk this woman came charging up to me beforehand and said, 'All right, big man, who's yer team up here?' I was in Glasgow so I thought the chances were she'd either be Rangers or Celtic and if I picked the wrong one I'd either get a Scotch kiss or a knee in the nuts.

'St Johnstone,' I said, backing away slightly just in case.

'Aaah, good for you,' she said.

Ever since then if I'm over the border I'll always pledge allegiance to St Johnstone, unless I'm in Dundee, of course. The two teams there fucking hate them. If I'm in Dundee I just say I've gone off the game.

You're always going to come unstuck sometimes, though, and if I had a quid for every time I'd put my foot in my mouth and said the wrong thing at a dinner I'd be a millionaire several times over. I once referred to the good people of Hartlepool as monkey hangers. Had I been in Manchester or even Middlesbrough I dare say I'd have got away with it but I wasn't, I was in fucking Hartlepool! Before you call me a stupid fat cunt I'd been told by a mate of mine that they took the whole thing as a joke and like a tit I believed him. The moment I said it, I knew I was in trouble, and it took all of my legendary charm to prevent them from lynching me. God knows what they'd have done if they had. Hanged me, most probably.

9

I Invented Robbie Williams

After I had my heart operation in 2020 I was staggered by the amount of people who got in touch to ask how I was. Some of the fuckers even wished me well! One of the most welcome messages was from a lanky Port Vale supporter who, back in the 1990s, was a very close friend of mine. He was in a boyband back then and once, after I decided it would be a good idea to kidnap him and take him with us on an end-of-season trip to Marbella, he got the sack. From then on life became unbearable for the poor bugger and I'm still riddled with guilt. Poor old Robbie Williams. Where the fuck did it all go wrong?

Like me, he's now a reformed character (actually, he's properly reformed whereas I'm working on it) and lives happily in LA with his family. After getting in touch and asking how I was, we ended up having a chat on Zoom for about an hour and a half. I'll tell you what, though, he's a handsome bastard. I'm sure he never used to be that good looking. You should have seen my missus. It was early morning where we were and night-time in LA and because of all this lockdown bollocks she hadn't had her roots done for a bit. Halfway through the chat Rob asked if he could say hello to Leah and she almost had a fit! Mr Fucking Smooth then went and told her she looked perfect so her legs turned to jelly. 'Robbie says I'm perfect, Robbie says I'm perfect!' I'll give him fucking perfect.

Once again, just like me Rob's had a few battles over the years but he's come out the other end. 'I've never been in a better place, Razor,' were his exact words. I found that quite inspiring, to be honest. I'm still at the start of my recovery so success stories like that are always welcome, not least because it's good to see mates – old and new – looking and feeling well. Do you know, he hasn't had a drink for over twenty years now? That's a good effort. Perhaps I'll do the same one day. Then again, perhaps Millwall will win the Champions League.

We finished off the chat by having a Neil Diamond singa-long. I came second in *Celebrity Stars in Their Eyes* once by sing-ing Neil Diamond's classic, 'Song Sung Blue'. I was beaten by some bird from *Emmerdale* singing Lulu. Fucking travesty! I thought that me having pretended to be Neil Diamond on tele-vision might have impressed me old mate Rob, especially as he's a singer, but he went one better.

'You're going to hate me for this,' he said, 'but when I lived in Malibu guess who my next-door neighbour was?'

I thought, you're having a fucking laugh, ain't yer! There's me thinking I'm the dog's whatsits because I've impersonated Neil Diamond in front of Matthew fucking Kelly and Williams has lived next door to him. After that we had a kind of Neil Diamond-off, where we each sang a line from one of his songs.

When we used to knock around together back in the 1990s Rob was a bit of a lump and he couldn't half put it back. In fact, while we were having this Zoom chat he reminded me of the fact that, back in the day, before we used to go out of an evening we'd each down a whole bottle of peach schnapps. It's not the volume of alcohol that bothers me, it's the fact that we were drinking peach fucking schnapps! He shouldn't have been in Take That, he should have been in the fucking Nolan Sisters and I should have been playing for Liverpool Ladies.

Anyway, at the end of the 1995–6 season me and some of the lads from the Liverpool dressing room decided to go to Marbella for a few days to unwind and, because Robbie had been hanging around with us quite a lot, we decided he should come with us. I forget who but one of us gave him a call and, instead of biting our hands off like we thought he would, he tried to blow us out. His excuse was that he was due in the recording studio with Take That so had to do as he was told.

'Balls to that,' I said to the lads. 'Let's kidnap the fucker.'

And that's exactly what we did. We booked him a ticket, turned up at his place a few hours before the flight, grabbed his passport, packed him a few clothes and then forced him on to the minibus. To be fair, he didn't put up much of a fight really so the word kidnap is probably pushing it a bit.

Anyway, at some point either during or just after the holiday, Robbie got sacked from Take That and the rest, as they say, is pop history. If it wasn't for me suggesting we ignore his initial refusal of our invitation and force him to come with us he might never have got the sack and if he hadn't been sacked we'd never have had 'Angels', 'Let Me Entertain You', a duet with Kylie – the lucky little fucker – and everything else the talented sod's done since. In fact, he would have nothing if it weren't for me getting him the sack. So, as per the title of this chapter, I invented Robbie Williams.

You're very welcome. Think nothing of it.

It doesn't stop there though. You see, I also invented Teddy Sheringham, in that I was responsible for him getting his break at Spurs. I can picture you all now shaking your heads and saying things like, 'What a load of bollocks,' but it's true. I'm a fucking legend, for God's sake. What do you expect? OK, let me give you a bit of background.

When I signed for Spurs for the second time in 1992 the manager, Terry Venables, in his infinite wisdom, decided to make me captain. That was probably one of the biggest compliments I'd ever been paid as a footballer but in addition to that I was also given the number six shirt which was the number Dave Mackay had worn as skipper during the club's glory days. I was God, basically, although humble with it.

Soon after making me captain the gaffer invited me into his office one day for a cup of tea. I had a feeling he was after some advice and, given my massive fucking brain and vast experience, he'd come to the right place.

'Yes, Terence,' I said, making myself comfortable on his chaise longue. 'What can I do for you?'

'I'm looking for a new striker,' he said, 'and I've got it down to a list of two – Teddy Sheringham and John Fashanu. What do you think, Razor? If you were me, which one would you sign?'

In my mind this was a fait accompli, as they say in French France. 'No disrespect to Fash,' I began, 'but I'm not sure he'd suit our style of football.'

'How so?' enquired the gaffer.

'Well,' I mused, 'Fash is used to playing all that route-one stuff. In fact, that's all he's ever played really, at Millwall and now at Wimbledon. Teddy Sheringham, on the other hand, is far more versatile and as well as being one of the best strikers I've ever played with he's also one of the most intelligent. Mark my words, gaffer,' I concluded, 'Teddy's your man.' A recommendation from yours truly, especially after mentioning the old intelligence bit, which seemed to impress him, was enough to seal the deal and within a few weeks Teddy was happily ensconced at White Hart Lane, where I understand he did rather well.

Seriously though, what a fucking player that boy was: 288 goals in 755 appearances and God knows how many assists. His spell at Man United was just incredible. Not only was he brought in to replace Cantona, the collar king, which can't have been easy, but he'd also lost a bit of pace by then and it could so easily have gone wrong. But what Teddy lacked in pace he more than made up for in the aforementioned brains, which, coupled with a shitload of natural ability, is ultimately what saw him through. Good-looking bastard too, and that's coming from one who knows.

Speaking of Mr Venables, which I just was, he came out with one of the best lines I've ever heard directed at a referee one day. It was during this second spell I was just alluding to and I'd just been involved in a scuffle with Crystal Palace's Andy Thorn that had resulted in me receiving a – wait for it – red bloody card. Given what had happened to me at Southampton the previous season you might think I'd been a bit foolish but on this occasion – as with so many others during my career – I was the victim of some appalling refereeing. This opinion was echoed by the gaffer who ran down from his seat in the stands after the incident to offer me some support.

'Unlucky, Raze,' he said as I walked off the pitch towards the tunnel. 'That was an appalling decision.'

This was only my third game since signing for Spurs and despite the decision being iffy I knew I'd get battered by the press. It was a case of my reputation coming before me. Sure enough, the press gave me an absolute walloping after the game, but when they turned their attentions to Terry he very kindly reiterated his opinion that the only person who'd let themselves down was the ref, which leads me nicely on to his line. When the press had cleared off Terry confronted the ref outside his office.

'Referee,' he said, 'if I called you a wanker, would I be in trouble?'

'Yes,' replied the ref.

'OK, what if I thought you were a wanker?'

'Well, no,' said the ref.

'In that case,' said Terry, 'I think you're a wanker.'

Fucking priceless! It was almost worth getting sent off to hear him say that.

But if Razor Ruddock invented Robbie Williams and Teddy Sheringham, which he did, among others, who the bloody hell invented Razor? That's a question many people have been asking themselves over the years and I pity the poor sod who gets the blame. Well, as far as this book is concerned that dubious honour goes to none other than Alan Shearer CBE, one of the nicest blokes you could ever wish to meet and, I'm proud to report, a very good mate, the thick Geordie twat.

The reason I'm blaming Shearer for my existence as a professional footballer is because it's all about him being shit and me being brilliant for a change, which is an opportunity I'm not prepared to let go. In fact, I'd like to shout this one from the rooftops. ALAN SHEARER WAS CAPABLE OF PLAYING LIKE A DICKHEAD!

The year was 1989 and I was playing for the Millwall reserve team, having been released by Spurs following my first stint there. The manager at Millwall at the time, John Docherty, was convinced that I should be playing as striker as opposed to a defender, so despite me having played as a defender for the last three years or so he insisted on sticking me up front. Because of this – and not to mention one or two other slight differences of opinion – it's safe to say that Mr Docherty and I weren't each other's biggest fans, and ever since joining the club again I'd been looking for a way out. This was a massive shame for me as Millwall were my club but you can't legislate for clashes of personality. It was just one of those things.

Anyway, one day – I think it was in February – we had the pleasure of playing Southampton reserves down at the Dell. John Docherty's assistant, my old mate Roger Cross, had decided to play me at the back for a change and before the match he had a word with me and asked me to mark a young wonderkid they had called Alan Shearer. 'No problem,' I said. 'You just leave the little fucker to me.'

Whether it was because I'd been playing out of position for so long and was keen to consolidate my place in defence I'm not sure, but from the moment the referee blew his whistle to start the game until the moment he blew it for full time, I battered Master Shearer from arsehole till fucking breakfast time. Honestly, he didn't know what had hit him. I even managed to break forward and score, which is more than he did. Anyway, the coaches from Southampton were so impressed by me putting their wonderkid to shame and making him look like he couldn't hit a barn door that they signed me the next day. What a turn up!

I suppose I could blame my general unhappiness at Millwall for the improved performance against Southampton but the fact remains that if Alan Shearer hadn't been so shit that day, I might never have been signed. Cheers Al!

Actually, while we're on the subject of Mr Shearer, or 'Shocksy', as we used to call him at Southampton, I have another little story that might make you laugh. The reason we used to call him Shocksy was because whenever he used to step up a level, either for Southampton or England, he would shock us all by doing something spectacular, like scoring a hat-trick against Arsenal, which he did on his full first-team Southampton debut. He was my first regular roommate at Southampton, who I joined in 1989, and because I used to feel a bit sorry for the dour little git I used to give him lifts here and there and lend him money. He was always skint in those days, or at least that's what he claimed.

'Oooh, av got nay brass, man,' he used to say. 'A canny get a roond in. Can ya lend uz a poond till pay day?'

That's right. He was Pakistani.

In truth, Shocksy's reputation for being a dour old fart is actually unfair because while he may appear to be grim, unfriendly, uncommunicative, ignorant, sour, bald, unkept and very, very boring, he's actually quite a nice bloke. And, I'm pleased to report, he likes the odd drink, which brings me nicely on to this story of mine.

Not for the first time, this particular story takes place on an end-of-season trip abroad and involves a certain amount of alcohol. The order of the day on the trip in question, which was to Portugal, by the way, was to get up reasonably early, play a round of golf, go to the beach for a swim and a perv, come back, have a few drinks, have a few more drinks and then go to somebody's bed. One night I went out on the town with Micky Adams, Matt Le Tissier and Elvis aka Barry Horne (Barry was an Elvis fanatic, hence the nickname). When we arrived back at the hotel the bar was packed so instead of trying to get a drink there we decided to retire to our rooms and empty our minibars. Within a couple of hours we'd managed to drink all four dry and after discovering that the bar was still jam packed we decided to think again.

'I know,' said Matt. 'Let's go and empty Shocksy's. He won't have touched any of it.' Back then, Shocksy hadn't yet found his drinking shoes so it was a good call.

'Let's go and knock him up then,' I said. 'He'll probably be asleep by now.' It was about 11 p.m. at the time and when we knocked on Shocksy's door we were half expecting him to appear in his pyjamas sucking his thumb. 'Fuck me,' I said when he finally opened up. He had a flannel over his privates and that was it. 'What are you up to?'

'A woz 'avin a fukin' bath, man,' said Shocksy before running off to jump back in. 'Anyway, wot do yerz want at this hoor? It's almost midnight! Shouldn't yerz be in bed?'

'We've come for your fucking minibar, son,' I informed him. By this time I'd already liberated a bottle of vodka and, as Elvis, Micky and Matt began the process of removing Shocksy's minibar from his room, complete with about twenty glasses on top of it, I decided to pour the vodka over Shocksy while he bathed. Why, I don't know. It just seemed like the right thing to do. Shocksy was shocked, it's fair to say, and he started to remonstrate.

'What the fukin' hell are ya doin' man?' he cried, trying to shield himself from the flowing spirit. 'Yuz gonna have t'pay for that man!' Just then, like a prick, he decided to look up and as he did some of the vodka went in his eye. 'YAAAAAAAAAAAAA MAN!' he screamed. 'YUV FUKIN' BLINDED US MAN! YUV FUKIN' BLINDED US!'

With the minibar now making its way through Shocksy's room door with the help of Matt, Elvis and Micky, it was time to leave. Unfortunately though, despite him having been partially blinded by an accidental round of vodka eyeballing, Shocksy caught sight of the absconding minibar and jumped out of the bath to give chase. 'COME BACK YER BASTADS!' he cried. 'GIVE US IT BACK MAN! GIVE IT BACK!'

With Shocksy now in tow, the speed of the escape stepped up a gear and as the Three Amigos wobbled down the corridor carrying Shocksy's minibar the glasses started falling to the floor and smashing behind them as they went. Just then, Shocksy came flying out of his room. He was obviously heading straight for the broken glass but before I could shout, 'Mind the glass!' he'd trampled straight on to it.

In my experience there's no sight more sobering than that of a mate who's lying on the floor screaming in agony having just walked through broken glass in bare feet. As you'd expect, there was blood absolutely everywhere and on closer inspection I could see that three of his toes had been cut to the bone and were hanging on by a thread. We obviously knew that we'd have to get him off to hospital immediately but there was one slight problem.

'Who hasn't been drinking?' I asked the others.

'Fuck knows,' said Micky. 'Shocksy's the only one who hasn't been on the piss, and he can't drive.' No shit Sherlock!

Even the coaching staff were hammered and the chances of getting an ambulance at that time of night in that location were zero.

'What about Steve Davis?' somebody finally suggested. 'I think he might be sober.'

After managing to track Steve down we discovered he was and so after lifting Shocksy into one of the hire cars I jumped in with him and Steve rushed us to the hospital. Well, I think it was a hospital. I'm not all together sure. Seriously, this place was like something from the 1880s. In fact, the only thing that persuaded you it wasn't was the fact it had electricity. Sometimes.

After being admitted Shocksy was put on a bed and wheeled into an open room. There were no curtains or chairs or anything. It was literally just a room with some sick people in it. By this time Shocksy had lost quite a bit of blood and he looked even more pale and confused than usual. 'You'll be all right son,' I reassured him. 'The doctor will be here soon'.

Just then he sat up and tried to speak. 'What were yuz doing with ma minibar man?' he whimpered. 'Woz yaz guin ta drink it in yaz room?'

'That's right, son,' I said, calming him down, having barely understood a fucking word. Geordie's difficult to understand at the best of times but when somebody's lost a lot of blood and has three toes hanging off you don't stand a fucking chance.

In all seriousness, I feared the worst for Shocksy's toes and was half expecting Florence Nightingale to appear carrying a lamp. Fortunately, the term 'never judge a book by its cover' appears to apply to hospitals in Portugal as about two hours later his toes were strapped up, having been sewn back on, and we were on our way back to the hotel. I chose not to ask how close he came to losing those three toes and, given what he went on to achieve with the help of them, I'd rather not know. Sometime after that, Shocksy finally found his drinking boots and I have it on good authority that if you ever try to nick his minibar these days you'll be in for a nasty surprise. Why? 'Coz al 'ave fukin' drunk it aaaal, man.' Yep, definitely from Pakistan.

10

Not All Footballers Are Thick
– Some Are Even Thicker!

When it comes to brains in sport, footballers, compared to the likes of rugby union players, have always been considered to be the poor relations. Or a bunch of thick over-paid wankers, as we're often known.

Like all generalisations, however, there will always be exceptions to the rule and this is no different. When asked by a newspaper about his views on education, Juan Mata once said, 'I don't think football and studying are mutually exclusive.' I have no idea what that means but it sounds good!

The fact is, though, that intelligence and football can go hand in hand – sometimes. Take the late Brazilian midfielder Sócrates, for example. Not only was he named after one of those clever bearded philosopher geezers from Greece who used to wear nothing but a bedsheet, but he also had a degree in medicine. The footballer that is, not the philosopher. Impressive, eh? Legend has it that old Sócrates studied in Ireland for a time and until recently he was believed to have played football for University College Dublin in the League of Ireland. That turned out to be a load of bollocks which, given the standard of Irish football in the 1970s, was a bloody good move. Leave it alone, son!

While we're on the subject of Ireland, my next exception to the rule of footballers being as thick as mince is the great Eamon Dunphy. Signed originally by Manchester United as an apprentice, Eamon failed to break into the first team at Old Trafford and after a loan spell at York City he ended up at my own beloved Millwall where he stayed for the best part of a decade, making 274 appearances. That alone makes him an absolute legend in my eyes but after hanging up his boots in the late 1970s Eamon had a go at journalism and it turned out he was just as good at kicking words around as he was balls. According to an article I read on the great man, Eamon is famed for his 'off-the-cuff remarks, his rapier-like wit and his talent for splitting audiences'. A man after my own heart then. It must be a Millwall thing.

Another former Millwall boffin, although just a loanee, is Glen Johnson. Did you know he studied for a maths degree while he was a player? It's true. It does leave me asking one question though. Given he must have studied angles and things during this degree of his, how come he used to take up the wrong defensive position so often? Just pulling your plonker, Glen. Top bloke.

But for every player who helps to disprove the myth that all footballers are knuckleheads there'll be one who reinforces it. My next example, although I love him dearly, is to brains what I am to healthy living. Ladies and gentlemen, boys and girls, I give you the lovely, but the not very brainy, Jason McAteer.

Liverpool signed Jason from Bolton in 1995 where his nickname in the dressing room had been Trigger. Unfortunately, my fellow defender Rob Jones had already been given that name so we had to think of something else. It would also have confused Jason no end having two Triggers in the dressing room and on some occasions he would have been forced to count to two. No, something had to be done. In the end we decided to stick with *Only Fools and Horses* and called him Dave after Rodney. This, when we tried to explain it, took Jason's confusion to new heights.

'Why am I called Dave when I should be called Rodney?' he used to ask. Well, at least he realised that the two names were different, which was a start.

One night we were all on the piss at a legendary nightclub in Dublin called Lillie's Bordello. We were quite far gone at the time but despite things being a bit blurry I spotted, out of the corner of my eye, the snooker legend Jimmy White. I fucking love a bit of snooker and with Jimmy being a south London boy I was all over it.

'Fucking hell, lads,' I said to the others, 'look over there. It's Jimmy White!'

'WAAAAAYYYYYYYYY' came the response. We were all completely twatted.

'I'll tell you what, lads,' I said, 'I'll go and ask him to join us.'

'WAAAAAYYYYYYYYY' they said again.

Pissed or not, I was starting to get fucking butterflies. It was Jimmy White!

'Right then,' I said, downing a cheeky shot for courage, 'I'll go and say hello.'

Just as I was setting off in the direction of the legend that is Jimmy White, Dave came stumbling over and pushed me out of the way.

'AAAAAAAAAYYYYYY, JIMMY!' he shouted at the top of his fucking voice. Even with all the noise Jimmy heard Dave's call and after recognising us he waved and began to come over. As Jimmy began his journey across the club Dave assumed the position of a snooker player mid-shot and, as Jimmy got within a few feet, Dave cried out the immortal words, 'ONE HUNDRED AND EEEEEEEEEEEIGHTY!'

What a fucking plonker, Rodney. Sorry, Dave. I get so confused.

Another time, Dave locked himself out of his Porsche one day. He'd left the keys in the ignition but despite the engine still running the car had locked itself.

'What am I going to do?' asked Dave.

'I don't fucking know. If the engine's running it shouldn't have locked itself, should it? Keep trying the door for a bit. And get a move on will ya? It's fucking freezing!'

We were outside his house at the time and were both wearing tracksuits. Because it was cold we had our hoods up and when Dave started trying to strongarm his car door open there's a small chance that we might just have looked a little bit suspicious. Two minutes later a police car drove past and sure enough, we did!

'What do you think you two are doing?' asked the policewoman. She was obviously expecting us to run off and looked surprised when we didn't.

'It's all right officer,' I said removing my hood. 'We're both footballers. Or at least I am. The car belongs to Dave and it's decided to lock itself.'

'With the engine running? Hey, he's not called Dave. He's called Jason!'

'It's a private joke, officer. Anyway, can you help him?'

Fortunately for us the policewoman was a Liverpool fan and seemed more than happy to oblige.

'Jason, would you mind going to get me a coat hanger please, love?' asked the policewoman.

'Yes, of course,' said Dave obediently.

About two minutes later Dave appeared with a coat hanger. A wooden coat hanger.

'What the fucking hell is she supposed to do with that, you lemon?'

'Hey, language, mister!'

'Sorry officer.'

I don't think I was her favourite player somehow. Had Fowler been there she'd probably have paid for a new key.

'No, Jason,' said the policewoman, as if talking to a thick dog, 'I mean a *wire* coat hanger.'

He looked at the wooden one in his hand and then at the car.

'Oh, right.'

The penny had finally dropped.

I could write a whole book about Dave. Anybody who makes me look vaguely normal deserves to have one written about them.

My favourite story regarding Dave took place in Ibiza. Me, him and about fourteen others hired a villa there once but after a couple of days we were bored stupid. The trouble was there were no birds so with five days still to go we decided to take action.

'Let's hire a bus, go down to the beach for the day, pick up some birds and come back for a party,' someone suggested (I can't think who). It sounded like a plan.

The following morning the bus turned up and we all piled on. After doing a head count I realised there was one missing.

'Hang on, lads,' I shouted. 'We're one short.'

I already had my suspicions as to who it was and after having another count up they were confirmed.

'Fucking hell, it's Dave. Where the hell is he?'

Just then the aforementioned locked Porsche owner jumped on the bus carrying a massive bag of ice.

'What the fucking hell are you doing with that?' I asked him.

'Ah,' said Dave tapping his forehead with a finger, 'you lot think I'm stupid, but I'm not. See this?' he said pointing at the ice. 'This is going to keep our drinks nice and cold all day. Now who's thick?'

'You fucking tit,' says I. 'The beach is half an hour away. It'll have melted by the time we get there.'

I could tell by the pained look on his face that he was trying to work something out.

'Oh yeah,' he said finally. 'I'll tell you what. I'll go and get another one.'

Once, when I ordered pizzas for us both, I asked Dave whether he wanted his cut into eight slices or four.

'Four please, Raze,' he said. 'I could never eat eight.'

What a fucking plonker!

While we're at Liverpool, Roy Evans wasn't exactly well endowed when it came to brains. Once, while trying to organise a match during a training session, he said, 'Us seven are going to play you five, in a twenty-minute five-a-side match lasting half an hour.' That said, he could also be very quick witted, could Roy. He once came into the dressing room at half time after having gone two-nil down. 'There are certain players in this dressing room who don't deserve to wear the red shirt of Liverpool,' he said.

'Care to name names?' I asked smugly

And without hesitation he pointed at me and said, 'Yes, you, you cunt.'

11

Nutters, the Lot of Them!

I suppose it's kind of inevitable that a book by someone like me will have a chapter about people who are a little bit unhinged. After all, it takes one to know one. Over the years I've met quite a few nutters and the ones I've spent time with have almost invariably ended up having a positive effect on my life. Not always on my career, but overall they're definitely in credit.

One of the funniest I've ever known is John 'Budgie' Burridge who was the first keeper I played with at Southampton. During his career Budgie played for over thirty different clubs and made over 750 appearances. His reputation went before him with regards to being a bit eccentric so by the time I arrived at the Dell I knew what to expect. Or at least I thought I did. No amount of words could have prepared me fully for what I experienced after meeting Budgie and I still can't believe some of the things he did. This is coming from a self-confessed bona fide fruitcake, by the way, so you'll know what to expect.

The first thing I noticed was the running commentary Budgie used to provide from the edge of the penalty box at every game. You'd receive the ball from him, turn away from goal and then suddenly hear his voice behind you. 'Burridge rolls it to Ruddock, who slips the ball through to Le Tissier, who . . .'

That's how he would go on for the entire match. The first time I heard him I smiled as I thought he was having a laugh. When I realised he wasn't I did a quick double take. I remember saying, 'What the . . .' He shouldn't have been wearing a jersey, he should have been holding a microphone and wearing a sheepskin coat!

You know when people do really silly things that stop you dead in your tracks? Well, this was one of those things. It made it impossible to concentrate, which is ironic really as it was obviously his way of maintaining concentration. What surprised me the most was the fact that even when he was involved in the action he'd carry on commentating and would shout things like, 'And that's another magnificent save by Burridge.' Another trait of his, which was obviously designed to put the fear of God into his back four, was shouting 'KEEPER'S . . .!' at the top of his voice when the ball was played over the top before following it up with '. . . NOT COMING!' He thought that was hilarious and providing you weren't on the receiving end I suppose it was.

It didn't stop there though. When he was at home Budgie would get his wife to throw oranges at him while he was sitting in the lounge wearing his goalkeeping gloves. He'd encourage her to throw them when he was least expecting it in order to improve his reflexes. That, my friends, was a sight to behold, believe me. Better still, he used to go to bed on a Friday night wearing his gloves and clutching a ball as a kind of pre-match ritual. What a complete and utter nutcase that man was, but what a character to have around the dressing room.

He was already about forty when I arrived at Southampton but he had the fitness of a man half his age. He was always either working or going through some routine. And he didn't drink. He didn't need to!

If you want eccentric, here's a story for you. One day Budgie turned up at the training ground carrying a three-foot-long steel rod and a set of six-inch nails, as you do. I mean, what else does a professional goalkeeper need? Before anyone could ask Budgie what he intended doing with the rod and nails he proceeded to pin the bar to the wall so he could do some pull-ups. I know this was thirty-odd years ago, but Southampton were a professional football club playing in the top division and had Budgie asked the club about purchasing some equipment that would have enabled him to do some pull-ups, I'm sure they would have obliged. Instead, Budgie had obviously decided to do things on his own. Not exactly the actions of a normal human being, but there we go. Budgie was anything but normal.

Once the bar was in place he decided to try it out but as opposed to reaching up and taking hold of it carefully just to make sure it would take his weight first, which might have been advisable, he decided to just jump up, grab hold and hope for the best. 'Don't be daft Budgie,' somebody said. 'If it comes off you'll do yourself a mischief.' Budgie being Budgie just ignored the advice and after dropping down into a squat position he jumped up and grabbled the pole with both hands. As he did so he let out a scream that would have woken the dead. At first we all thought he was joking but then he started shaking violently and screaming at the top of his voice.

'Fuck me, he's being electrocuted,' shouted one of the coaches. 'Somebody get the electricity turned off, now! And for God's sake, don't touch him.'

Do you know what the dickhead had done? He'd only gone and hammered one of his nails straight through an electricity cable. Poor old Budgie was properly shaken up by it but he recovered. It played havoc with his hair though. He looked like a white Don King.

Unfortunately, Budgie left Southampton at the end of that season so the dressing room lost a big character. Luckily though, as one nutcase exited the dressing room (having almost killed himself) another one entered, and although he wasn't quite as eccentric as Budgie he had one character trait that kept us all in stitches. The character in question is Barry 'Elvis' Horne who I'm happy to say became a big mate of mine. When he first arrived I thought he was quite normal but my opinion quickly changed about halfway through a pre-season trip to Portugal.

It happened to be Barry's birthday while we were there and, having celebrated in the usual way by having one or two halves of shandy, I was charged with helping a decidedly worse-for-wear Barry back to his room. The journey up there was awful. I don't know what he's like now but Barry used to be quite an energetic sort of drunk and as we made our way through reception and down the various corridors he kept on attempting to do flying headers. I said, 'For fuck's sake, Elvis, will you just calm down! You're going to hurt yourself.' When we finally reached his room he was still jumping about like Keith Chegwin on speed so I allowed him one free header before bed. 'After that though, I'm off, all right?'

Hanging in the middle of his room was a round lampshade that appeared to be made of fabric. It was roughly the size of a football so seemed perfect. 'You see that there,' slurred Elvis. 'Am gonna fuckin' head that. Watch this.'

I didn't want to really, but I had no choice.

After running to the far end of the room Elvis turned, ran back and launched himself at the lampshade. I have to say it was a magnificent header and had it been on a football pitch with an actual football I dare say he'd have won himself a nice round of applause. Except it wasn't a football pitch, it was a hotel room, and the lampshade that looked like a football definitely wasn't. It was a piece of fabric that happened to be wrapped around a large lump of solid steel.

Poor old Elvis. The noise I heard when he made contact with the lampshade was obviously unexpected and the only thing I can compare it to is when you strike one of those hammer bell things at a fairground, just without the bell!

'Jesus Christ, Elvis,' I said, running to his aid. 'Are you OK?'

'I think so,' he said, rubbing his head. 'I feel a bit dizzy though. And I think I'm bleeding.'

'I'm not surprised. You've just headed a ball of fucking steel, you great tit.'

He had to have four stitches and by the time I relinquished responsibility of him I was stone-cold sober. Barry went on to get a first class honours degree from the University of Liverpool in chemistry. How the fuck did that happen?

One of the biggest characters I ever came into contact with in the Spurs dressing room was Steve Sedgley. I also played alongside Steve for England Under-21s and he's about two weeks younger than I am. Like Budgie, Sedge was absolutely off his rocker and he specialised in playing pranks on people. I can remember being woken up in the middle of the night by Sedge prior to an away game. We were in a hotel and he was knocking on my door. It must have been about two o'clock in the morning. 'Help!' he cried while banging on the door. I remember thinking, *Should I answer that or shouldn't I?* When it came to pranks Sedge's currency of choice was shock value and he'd given people nightmares in the past.

'Aww, fuck off Sedge,' I said eventually. 'I don't know what you're up to but I'm trying to get some sleep. Go back to bed.'

As opposed to getting rid of him this just made him worse and his cries for help went up a notch, as did his bangs on the door. 'HEEEEEEELP!' he screamed. 'RAZOOOOOOOR, HEEEEEEEELP! I'M DYING.'

'Oh, for fuck's sake,' I said rolling out of bed. 'Hang on, I'll be there in a second.'

After having a quick pee I walked to the door, took hold of the handle, closed my eyes and braced myself. After pulling the door open I slowly opened my eyes. On reflection I wish I hadn't as nothing could have prepared me for what was standing in front of me. Sedge was stark bollock naked and he appeared to have something hanging out of each nostril. He was also screaming in agony so whatever they were they were obviously making him feel a bit uncomfortable.

'What the fucking hell have you got hanging out of your nostrils, Sedge?' I snapped. 'You look fucking ridiculous.

'IT HURTS, RAZE,' he shouted, jumping up and down. 'IT HURTS!'

Instead of continuing this in the corridor I decided to bring him inside and, after chucking him a towel and asking him to cover himself up, I sat him down and began my investigation as to what was protruding from his hooter. It didn't take long, and after reaching my conclusion I presented Sedge with the evidence.

'Why the fuck have you got a wine gum sticking out of each nostril?' I asked.

Sedge looked at me as though he had no idea they were there and after running over to the mirror he pulled them out one by one, put them in his mouth and started chewing.

'You, my son, are a fucking loon,' I deduced.

Just then Sedge moved one of his hands as if to scratch his arse and after leaning forward he stood up straight suddenly and held out his hand.

'Have you just pulled something out of your arse?' I ask somewhat gingerly.

It looked like another wine gum but before I could ask Sedge he popped it in his mouth and, as before, started chewing. I couldn't believe my eyes!

He then said, 'Thanks a lot, Raze,' and after throwing me the towel I'd given him he ran to the door, opened it and buggered off, like Wee Willie Winkie!

He never mentioned this incident to me and I certainly didn't mention it to him, but I later found out – this was after I'd left Spurs – that he'd bought the wine gums especially *and* had ordered the wake-up call for 2 a.m. just to see my reaction.

But it wasn't just teammates who used to bear the brunt of Sedge's strangeness, opponents did too. I remember seeing Paul Merson in his car at some traffic lights once. He was driving home from the Arsenal training ground, and me and Sedge were in my car driving back from the Spurs training ground. On seeing Merse, Sedge suddenly cried 'STOP!' and before I could ask him what the hell he was up to he started stripping off as if his life depended on it. There are certain situations when it's best not to ask questions and to let nature take its course, like when a dog bites your leg. This was one of those occasions so while Sedge got into his birthday suit I just sat there, blew my horn and tried to attract the attention of Merse.

I needn't have bothered because a few seconds later Sedge leapt from the car and sprinted towards an oblivious and unsuspecting Merse. The area was absolutely full of pedestrians and cars, and within seconds of him emerging people started shouting at him to cover himself up. They must have thought he'd escaped from a lunatic asylum or something. On reaching Merse's car Sedge banged on his window, stood back and started waving at him. 'Hiya, Merse!' he shouted at the top of his voice. 'How are you mate? Good to see ya.' Merse was in absolute stitches and when the lights turned to green he pulled over.

Sedge was in no mood to chat though and after finding a stray bollard he placed it on the side of the road, perched himself on top and started waving at Merse and all the passing traffic. That is, to this very day, one of the most bizarre situations I've ever found myself in, and I'm sure Merse would say the same. Not Sedge though. That's normality to him.

12

Come on Ref, You're Having a Laugh!

My relationship with refs was always a bit up and down, and because I was a big character with a big gob the men in black usually either loved me or loathed me. It wasn't always that simple though. Take Keith Hackett, for instance. He, like Roger Milford, was one of the few refs I could have a bit of banter with and despite the odd word being exchanged between us now and then we seemed to have an understanding. You can imagine my surprise then, when, about twenty years ago, I picked up a Sunday newspaper one day only to find an article written by Keith about players he didn't like entitled 'The Gobfathers', in which I had a starring role. It was actually me, Paul Ince and Bryan Robson who had incurred Keith's wrath and, boy, did he go to town on us all! He accused Paul Ince of being mouthy (!) and claimed that I always had to have the last word. I can only put it down to the fact that he must have needed some new earrings or something so decided to sell his soul. I was very hurt by that, Keith. Last word indeed!

Come to think of it, I do remember something that relates to me having the last word. It was one of Keith's last ever games, I think, so the article must have been written just after he retired. It was at Old Trafford and after awarding us a penalty he spotted the linesman's flag and decided to change his decision and award them a free kick. On that occasion I do seem to remember questioning Keith's sanity and also, as I probably have done with every referee over the years, not to mention most players, his parenthood. He definitely bottled it though. The useless bastard!

My reputation used to go against me with refs and because that reputation wasn't entirely unfounded I suppose I'm to blame. Fuck me, am I being magnanimous here? That makes a change. In my defence, I was only sent off five times in my career, although I have a feeling that my reputation for being a bad'un had almost as much to do with my behaviour off the pitch as it did on it. Take Francis Benali, for instance, my old teammate at Southampton. He neither drank nor smoked and always went to bed straight after *Coronation Street*. He was also very mild mannered so, despite the fact that he was a dirty little fucker who got over twice as many red cards during his career than I did, he rarely came in for any stick from refs. Bless his cotton socks! Then again, I'd much rather go out and enjoy myself, play the game my way and go into battle with a ref once in a while than sit at home drinking tea. Each to their own.

In an attempt to counter this reputation of mine — at least when it came to the refs — I used to go out of my way to have a laugh and joke with them before a match. You know the kind of thing, pinch their nuts or pretend to stick one on them, stuff like that. I didn't do it so they'd treat me differently, I did it so they'd treat me fairly. Although looking back perhaps pinching somebody's bollocks or pretending to give them a Scotch kiss isn't the best way to go about winning them over and persuading them you're actually not a thug.

Most of them would have a laugh and joke with me before-hand, but the moment we got on the pitch everything would change. Apart from the aforementioned Roger Milford. He was cut from a very different cloth to other blokes and was the only referee I could get away with calling a cunt during a game. I remember I was playing for Southampton away at Arsenal and sometime during the second half Roger made a mistake. I said, 'Roge, you cunt. You're having a fucking nightmare!'

'Come here, son,' he said, beckoning me over to him. I thought, *Shit, I might have gone too far here.* 'You see that score-board,' he said pointing to it. 'That says Arsenal three Southampton one. I'm not the cunt having a nightmare, son, you are. Now fuck off!'

I remember him standing there with his mop of curly hair and tan. He looked like a heartthrob from *Crossroads*. I love old Roge. He used to make me piss myself.

Little Brian Hill was another character. I remember running up to him during a match once and saying, 'What the fucking hell were you doing there, ref?'

He just looked at me and said, 'Oh yes, I'm sorry about that. I'll tell you what, why don't you have a go?' and then he handed me his whistle. Talk about taking the wind out of my sails. I felt like a right prick. Brian Hill, the only man ever to make Razor Ruddock shut his gob.

When players' surnames first went on the back of shirts I got collared by a ref at Anfield and, after taking out his yellow card, he said, 'Turn around, Ruddock.' Then, after deliberately studying the name on the back of my shirt he wrote it on the card in front of forty-five thousand people. I could hear the laughter coming from every bloody stand, and from the pitch! I felt like a naughty schoolboy, which was obviously the desired effect. It was bloody brilliant.

I don't know if there was one ref in particular who spoiled that relationship between them and the players but the one who springs to mind is – surprise surprise – David Elleray. The closest I got to having a conversation with him on the pitch was when he booked me at Palace once. I said something along the lines of, 'Really, Mr Elleray, that was an outrageous decision,' or words to that effect, and he just smiled and said, 'Yes, possibly, but I can't wait to tell me mates I booked you.' Again, that took the wind right out of my sails and, to be fair to the bloke, I probably behaved myself for the rest of the match.

I'm often asked if it was ever possible to intimidate or influence referees and the short answer is yes, but especially at Anfield, and especially in front of the Kop. That certainly used to intimidate referees, which in turn could influence their decisions. I remember playing a game there once when Jeff Winter was refereeing. Despite the David Ellerays of this world imposing a headmaster-type discipline on the field of play, you could still have a laugh with Jeff and we've gone on to become really good mates. During this game we'd just had a corner and when the ball went out for a goal kick me and Jeff started arguing about something. I forget what. We then started running back towards the halfway line and instead of paying attention to the game we carried on our spat. Suddenly, out of the blue, my fellow Liverpool players started appealing for a penalty. I looked at Jeff and said, 'What you gonna do?' knowing full well that he hadn't seen a thing.

'Well,' he said, 'the Kop didn't appeal, did they?' He then blew his whistle and said, 'No penalty!'

The players all looked at me as if to say, 'What the fuck's going on?' so I just shrugged my shoulders.

Julian Dicks went in two-footed on Perry Groves once at Upton Park and Perry went fucking mental. 'Ref,' he shouted, 'send him off! He almost fucking killed me!'

The ref just said, 'If you think I'm sending him off here, you've got another think coming!' and then he ran off.

Another time I was at the bar in the Swallow Hotel at Waltham Abbey when all of a sudden Jeff walked in. 'Hello, Jeff,' I said. 'Fancy a drink?'

'Aye, just a small one though. I'm reffing a game tomorrow.'

A little while later I suggested to Jeff that we pop around to a boozer, run by Terry Venables's dad, which was just around the corner. 'I had no idea Terry's dad had a boozer,' he said in his Teesside brogue. 'Go on then,' he said. 'Just the one mind.'

'Of course, Jeff,' I said. 'Just the one!'

I got him absolutely shitfaced. I got him on the karaoke, puking up, the works. I even had to carry him back to his room. What a night we had! The next morning he called me up and said, 'What the fucking hell did you do to me, you horrible bastard? I've got to referee a game today!'

'Yeah,' I said. 'Good luck with that.'

I love Jeff to bits, the miserable little turd.

13

We're Playing for Ingerland – Ingerland!

While we're on the subject of my considerable reputation occasionally coming before me – and usually biting me on the arse – which I have to admit still happens quite a bit, the most worry it's ever given me is when, in 1994, I was called up for the senior England squad for a match against the United States.

I was at York races when I got the news. Me and my fellow Liverpool players had decided it was time for a day out and with the majority of us being keen on the gee-gees this seemed like a good idea. As you'd expect, the beer and wine had been flowing from about breakfast time and by the time the first race was announced we were all pretty cheerful. Shortly after the first race had finished an announcement came over the Tannoy. 'Would Mr Neil Ruddock – that's Mr Neil Ruddock – please come to the information desk as soon as possible? There is an urgent message for you.'

Despite smartphones not having been invented yet we did have mobiles so after checking that mine was working I figured that whoever was trying to get hold of me couldn't have been family or even a friend. So who the hell was it then? As I stumbled down to the information desk all sorts of things were going through my head, and none of them good. As I said, because of my reputation – and occasionally my behaviour – controversy tends to follow me around quite a bit and as I walked on I kept wracking my brains trying to think of anything I'd done that could merit an 'urgent message'.

When I reached the information desk I smiled defeatedly at the woman on duty and uttered the immortal words, 'Hello, I'm Neil Ruddock. What have I done?' The woman gave me a look that said, 'Ooh, hello. You're a bit pissed,' and then handed me a piece of paper. I refused it on account of seeing six of everything and I asked her to read it out.

'With pleasure, sir. Mr Terry Venables rang. You've been called up for the England squad. You're to report to Bisham Abbey first thing tomorrow morning.'

The woman then gave me another look that said, '*You've been called up for the England squad? God help England!*' She actually had a point.

This forced me to do something that until then I honestly didn't think would be possible. Abandon a day on the piss, go home, sober up and get a nice early night. It was all temporary but the effect it had on me in the immediate sense was life changing. There is no greater compliment as a footballer than being called up for your country and when I left my house the following morning – carrying about ten packets of mints which I hoped would mask the smell of alcohol – I felt on top of the world. Well, mentally. Physically I was a wreck.

Unfortunately, I only made the bench for that match against the United States but just being involved was enough for me. Seriously! I was obviously desperate to play but the atmosphere was so relaxed and so friendly that, on that first occasion at least,

I honestly didn't care. I was just very happy to be there. Working with Terry again also played a big part in my enjoyment and even when I was called up for the next two matches but remained on the bench I didn't really mind. By then, I felt like part of the squad almost and I knew I had to be patient. It doesn't matter how many times you get called up, if the manager doesn't think you're good enough or are the right man for the job, you won't get on. There's no divine right.

The matches I was called up for were all friendlies but Euro '96 was just eighteen months away at the time and because I was part of the current England squad I allowed myself to dream about making it to the competition. In fact, it became my goal, as I'm sure it did every player who was either in or on the fringes of every international squad vying to qualify.

My original dream of actually playing for my country came true on 16 November 1994. The match in question was against Nigeria and although it was another friendly it made absolutely no difference to me. A cap's a cap. What really excited me at the time was the thought of being referred to as Neil Ruddock of Liverpool *and* England. My mum was in tears when I told her and even my old man and my two brothers might have had a moment each. I had several! It was what I had always dreamed of and it was only when I started telling my family and friends that it really began to sink in.

The reason I got the call to play was because the regular centre halves, Tony Adams and Gary Pallister, were both injured and so me and Steve Howey stepped up to replace them. But, as well as being the reason for me winning my first England cap, Tony and Gary were also the reason why I never won another. They were just about the best in the business at the time and although I'd have loved to have won more caps for England, being kept out by those two is definitely no disgrace.

Steve and I found out we'd be starting the game on the Monday before, which gave us a few days to get used to playing alongside each other. Had the manager told us the day before the match I'd have been a bundle of nerves. Yet again, Mr Venables got it absolutely spot on and come the day of the match I was quite relaxed. Nervous, but relaxed. His approach to the build up for a game was second-to-none in my experience as not only would he tell you exactly how to do your job properly but he'd make you aware of what your opponent was likely to do and how to combat it. He always seemed to think of everything, and that in itself used to inspire confidence. Until I played for him at Tottenham during my second spell at the club I'd never been coached like that before and it made me approach the game differently. He used to make me visualise certain things – situations mainly – and then we'd talk about how I'd sort them out. I'd visualise the solutions too and after a while it became second nature. It also goes without saying that Terry was a great motivator and even though the Nigeria game I played in was 'just another friendly' en route to Euro '96, he left me in no doubt that it was much more than that.

The match itself was quite a lively affair and although Nigeria were fancied we ended up nicking it 1–0. That goal should have been mine and, had it not been for David Bloody Pratt Platt nipping in front of me at the near post I'd have been the hero of the night. As the ball came in, courtesy of a Dennis Wise cross on the right, I remember thinking, 'This is mine,' only for this short Lancastrian bloke to nip in, poach the goal, as he often did, and steal all the glory.

Was I really bothered? Not really. It would have been nice, I suppose, but I'm not sure my nerves would have taken it. I don't remember this but according to a mate of mine called Danny who lived in Hornchurch I looked as white as a sheet when I ran on to the pitch before the game. No, putting on an England shirt, walking up the tunnel at Wembley and playing for my country in front of eighty thousand people was enough excitement for one night, thank you very much.

My favourite part of the night was spotting my mum and dad in the crowd as we walked up to the halfway line for the national anthem. That was yet another 'moment' and I do believe I may have had to take a deep breath or two. Gets yer right here, dunnit?

I spoke to Terry after the match and he was happy with my performance. As well as telling me to work hard on my fitness he gave me the impression that, providing I did as I was told and kept my nose clean, there'd be no reason why I wouldn't be given another runout. Receiving praise and encouragement like that from someone like Terry Venables is a proper shot in the arm and I don't mind admitting that I went back to the north-west with a bit of a spring in my step. If it happened again, brilliant, but if it didn't, do you know what, that was fine too. It was the fact that I'd performed well for my manager and my country and was in the reckoning – that's really what put a smile on my face.

Unfortunately, by the time it came to Terry choosing his squad for the next England friendly I was injured. I came back, of course, but I was never the same player after that and I lost a bit of consistency. I did captain the England B team for a match against the Republic of Ireland, but that was as close as I got to the full squad again. Come on, get your fucking violins out! It's tragic, innit? Anyway, I've got a cap for England and have played at Wembley and you haven't, so you can piss right off!

If I could give anybody who is in that situation where you're striving for a dream one piece of advice – in addition to never losing sight of that dream – it would be to manage your expectations. Getting carried away from time to time's all well and good, and if we didn't allow our imaginations to run away with us occasionally we wouldn't be human, but by managing your expectations – or at least trying to – you'll be saving yourself a lot of heartache and upset. I don't think I was ever taught how to manage my own expectations. It was something I just picked up, from my dad, I think. He probably never realised he was doing it but nevertheless it's something I'll always be grateful for.

I'll tell you what, how about a quick Gazza story before we move on? One of the things I was most looking forward to after joining the England squad was spending a bit of time with Gazza, partly because he was such a legendary player, of course – even the thought of playing in the same team as him made me itch a bit – but also because I wanted to see if he was as mad as everyone said he was. All right, let's be honest. That's what I was really looking forward to! I wanted to see Gazza at his berserk best and I wasn't disappointed.

There's a misconception about Gazza that all his antics off the pitch involve booze, but that's not the case. Yes, we all know he likes a drink, but Gazza's unnerving unpredictability was with him from birth I reckon. In fact, I'm sure it was. Anyway, to prove that alcohol wasn't always the main instigator he invited some of the new crop of lads to the cinema one afternoon and fortunately I was one of them. Some of the more established squad members came along too and all in all there must have been about fifty of us. I forget why but we arrived at the cinema about an hour early for the film we were seeing and after grabbing a drink – a soft drink, I might add – Gazza and I sneaked into the auditorium.

The previous showing had finished and there was a team of people busily cleaning up all the popcorn and what have you. As opposed to just leaving them to it, Gazza decided to give them a hand, with his gob.

'Get a fuckin' move on, yer lazy bastads,' he shouted. When they all looked up and realised who he was, he smiled and gave them a thumbs up. 'Only jokin' wi yerz. Yer lazy bastads!'

It must have been the Gazza effect as after calling them all lazy bastards – twice – the work rate seemed to speed up and within ten minutes or so the place was absolutely spotless.

'You can take your seat now,' said one of the members of staff. 'The doors are about to open.' At this point I looked round to find Gazza but he was nowhere to be seen so the member of staff had just been talking to me. Just then the door opened and in shuffled the rest of the players, but again, no Gazza. As they all headed towards the seats I suddenly heard his unmistakable voice and a few second later he appeared. He was carrying not one but two gigantic buckets of popcorn.

'Wahey ladz!' cried Gazza. 'Popcorn's on me man!'

The members of staff were all standing in a line watching Gazza perform and for people who had just spent twenty minutes or so picking up popcorn they didn't seem to be that concerned about the mad Geordie carrying two overflowing buckets of it. I was! I knew he was up to something, I just didn't know what.

'Come on, Gazza,' I said almost paternally. 'Let's go and sit down, shall we?'

'Howay and shite man! Aaaah, gan on then. I'll go first.' As Gazza walked past me he made out as if I'd tripped him up and as me and the members of staff watched on in horror he threw himself and his two buckets of popcorn theatrically to the floor. It was a performance that Wilfried Zaha himself would have been proud of and when Gazza hit the floor all the players – minus myself, of course – started cheering. That wasn't the end of Gazza's performance though. Far from it. It was time for him to be outraged.

'What the fuck der yer think yer wuz doing man?' he cried at the top of his voice while pointing at me. 'Did yer see that?' he said, addressing the members of staff. 'That man deliberately tripped me up. Yuz all saw it, didn't yuz? I think you owe these people an apology, Mr Ruddock. Yer a disgrace to yer country and the badge.'

What made this even more astonishing was that Gazza was injured at the time so he probably shouldn't have been at the cinema, and he definitely shouldn't have been throwing himself on the floor while carrying two buckets of popcorn, the mad Geordie bastard.

While we're here I think I should give you my theory as to why the England team never seem to realise their full potential. And yes, I know we got through to the semis of the World Cup in 2018, but who did we have to beat to get there? Tunisia, Panama, Colombia – just – and Sweden. Not one of them are what you'd call first division.

In my humble opinion, one of the reasons the players can't get it together for the national team the same way they do for their domestic teams is the reception they receive when they underperform. If Marcus Rashford has a shit game for Man United he'll still get clapped off at the end of the game, and it's the same with all the other players. Unless their team is fighting relegation, which is unlikely, or is on a particularly poor run of form the chances are they're not going to get much grief from the supporters. When you're playing for England it's a very different kettle of fish and if you lose or have a shocker there'll be up to ninety thousand people telling you it's not good enough. It's obviously not the players' fault but if they're used to being venerated even when they lose and then go and play for England, whose fans are hard taskmasters, it is going to be potentially terrifying. But it's not just the game itself and the potential result that must be daunting for the players. You've got the build-up too. They must think, *Shit, if we lose here we're going to get hammered by the fans and the press.* Losing for your club is never good, but it's a lot worse losing for your country. You remember when we got beat by Iceland? That game, which unfortunately has been etched into my memory for all eternity, is a case in point as nobody wanted the ball. And why did nobody want the ball? Because they were shit scared of losing it.

Everybody probably has a theory as to how much of a footballer's success is down to talent and how much of it is down to mental strength. All I can say from my own experience – both watching and playing football – is that you can have all the talent and skill in the world but if you don't have what it takes to put it into practice – which includes being able to play in difficult situations and being able to block out England supporters giving you a hammering when you lose to a shit team – then it's useless. Well, not useless, but you see what I mean. What's the good in playing well for your club and winning caps for your country when you can't do yourself justice for the latter. Even the Lampards and the Gerrards of this world used to suffer from this, and you remember when Wayne Rooney got taken off at half time because the England fans were giving him a hard time? What's frustrating for me, and I'm sure for the fans and the press, is that sometimes this mental block disappears and it all comes together, but it doesn't happen often enough. Also, it seems to be the poorer the opposition the poorer we play.

Sort it out somebody!

14

There Are More Things
in Heaven and Earth

S ome of you will think this is a load of old bollocks but a few
years ago our house became haunted by a perverted ghost
called George who had a bit of a thing for my missus. We
managed to get him to sling his hook in the end with the help
of a well-known medium but not before he'd caused havoc.

It all started about five years ago when Leah said that she'd
felt a presence in the bedroom while she was getting undressed.
Now before you start jumping to conclusions I wasn't in the
house at the time and it was the window cleaner's day off, so
whatever it was she sensed wasn't me or him. Joking aside, it
really did freak her out and when I got home she was in a right
state. Even so, I was more than a little bit sceptical when she
told me what had happened although I did try my best and
humour her a bit.

'There's no such thing as ghosts, you blonde twonk,' I said
lovingly. 'Pull yourself together. You probably left a window
open or had wind or something.'

My words of comfort didn't have the desired effect unfortunately and over the next few weeks she kept droning on about it.

'I'm telling you, Razor, I can feel somebody looking at me,'
she'd say. 'It's horrible. I don't feel safe in my own home.'

Despite being sceptical the last thing I wanted was an unhappy wife so in the end I asked the medium, Derek Acorah, who had been on Liverpool's books for a time before suffering a really bad injury and was a friend of a friend, if he'd come down and investigate.

When Derek arrived I did my best to take it seriously and tried not to laugh. It wasn't easy though. I find it hard keeping a straight face at the best of times but when somebody claims they're being leered at by a perverted ghost only one thing's going to happen I'm afraid. After showing Derek around the house, Leah and him sat down to chat and while they did I tried to keep out of the way.

'You don't believe Leah do you, Razor?' shouted Derek from the other room.

I'd been rumbled.

'It's not that I don't believe her, Derek,' I said, trying to sound convincing. 'I just think it's a complete load of old bollocks!' I'm sorry, but I couldn't keep it up any more. 'Look,' I said, 'I haven't seen or sensed a thing since all this started and at the end of the day I don't believe in it.'

Derek was obviously used to dealing with sceptics but as I talked I could tell he was becoming annoyed.

'Leah's not making it up, Razor,' he said. 'There is a spirit in this house and he's infatuated with her.'

Once again I started to laugh.

'Do you want me to prove it to you?' said Derek.

'Yeah, go on then,' I replied. 'What are you going to do, bring him on for the second half or something?'

Derek stood up.

'Come with me, Razor,' he said.

'What, am I for the naughty step?'

I must admit at being a tiny bit spooked by this, pardon the pun.

'Where are we going?' I asked him.

'You're going up to your bedroom,' he said. 'I want you to go in there and turn on the light.'

Turn on the light? I thought you were supposed to turn off the lights when you went looking for ghosts?

'Once you've done that just stand there for a few minutes.'

I did as I was asked and went up to our bedroom and after turning on the light I sat down on the edge of the bed. I wasn't going to stand there like a lemon! I thought, I'll give it two minutes just to keep him happy and then go down. I looked around the room and, as expected, I couldn't hear or sense a thing. If we did have a perverted ghost in the house he definitely didn't like fat blokes in their later forties.

Now you can take the piss out of me all you like, but just before I stood up to go downstairs again somebody said 'Hello' in my left ear. I swear I'm not shitting you. This actually fucking happened.

'Who the hell's that?' I said jumping across the bed. I was up and out of that room in about two seconds flat. 'Fuck me,' I said after closing the door. My heart was going like the shithouse door when the plague's in town. I couldn't believe it.

When I found Derek and Leah in the living room they were both smiling.

'You've met George then,' said Derek.

'George?' I said. 'Who the fuck's George?'

'George is your resident ghost,' explained Derek.

This was getting weirder and weirder.

'Tell George from me he's a fucking pervert,' I said.

According to Derek, George the perv was a dead soldier who'd been shot down during the Second World War. This actually made some sense as a lot of Spitfires had been downed over Kent during the Battle of Britain. It didn't explain him being a pervert though!

Despite George the perv having apparently whispered a quick hello in my lughole I still only half believed it and by the next day I'd managed to convince myself that I'd been imagining things. Then, that evening, while Leah and me were watching the box, one of five wooden ornaments we had hung on the wall suddenly fell to the floor and before either of us could say anything another one went. Now I fucking believed it!

'JESUS CHRIST,' I said, jumping out of my seat. 'For fuck's sake Leah, call Derek!'

The following night one of our dining-room chairs started wobbling, which shit me right up, and fortunately Derek arrived the day after. I was that spooked by it all that I decided to make myself scarce and when I got back Derek assured me that George the perv had been given his marching orders.

'How'd you manage that then?' I asked.

'I shouted at him,' said Derek.

'You what? You shouted at a ghost?'

'That's right.'

I honestly didn't care any more. I just wanted the house back to ourselves.

The two or three days after Derek left were a bit nervy as every time we heard a noise we thought it was George but by the following weekend we hadn't heard from him so we assumed he'd done as he was told and buggered off.

Do you know what this reminds me of? That episode of *Only Fools and Horses* where Uncle Albert gets Elsie Partridge to hold a seance at the Nag's Head. I absolutely love that programme and funnily enough that's one of my favourite episodes. My favourite part is when Rodney – or should I say Dave? – starts talking about reincarnation and comes out with the immortal line, 'If there is such a thing as reincarnation, knowing my luck I'll come back as me!' It gets me every time that does. What a nightmare that would be though – Razor Ruddock, the sequel! Too scary.

So, after all that do I believe in ghosts now? To be honest, I'm still not really sure but I'm keeping an open mind. As the title of the chapter goes, there are more things in heaven and earth, my old son.

15

What a Pranker

While I'm on the subject of getting spooked in your own home . . .

Me and Alan Shearer used to live on the same road in Formby, which is a posh part of Liverpool. How I came to be accepted into the area I have no idea but we had a lot of fun while we were there. We used to play golf all the time and sometimes, if he could find his Post Office book, me and him would go and have a pint afterwards. Alan's wife used to go back to Southampton quite a lot, which is where she comes from, and when that happened we used to hook up.

During one such occasion we'd arranged to meet up for a pint one day during the week but when I rang him up to set a time he'd changed his mind.

'Oh, come on, you tart,' I said to him. 'I'm fucking gasping here. I'll see you down the pub in ten.'

'Nah, man,' he said. 'Av decided to stay in like.'

'You what?' I replied. 'Staying in? What do you mean you're staying in? Come on. The missus is away. Let go and have a couple of jars. You know it makes sense.' I genuinely thought I had him by this time but apparently not.

'Nah, man. Av decided to stay in and watch *Crimewatch* instead. You can gan by yerself if yer like.'

'I know I can gan by myself but I don't want to gan by myself do I? I want to gan with you!' He was getting on my tits now.

'Nah,' he said defiantly. 'Av made up me mind, man. See yerz later.' And with that he put the phone down.

Alan Shearer developing a mind of his own was a scary fucking concept but there was nothing I could do. Or was there? After giving it some thought I figured that if he was going to stay in and watch *Crimewatch*, which, let's face it, was always a bit scary on your own, I would try and make the occasion that little bit scarier. After all, we were mates, and if you can't do something for a mate, what can you do?

After asking for a pair of my now ex-wife's tights I put them over my head, ran up the road and jumped over his gate. As I ran up the drive I could see there was a gap in his living-room curtains so after sneaking up to the window I carefully looked through the gap and peered in. He was lying on his settee watching *Crimewatch* as promised. He was wearing nothing but a pair of boxer shorts and had one hand down the front of them while the other was clutching a bag of crisps. 'Right then, Mr Shearer,' I said under my breath. 'Heeeeeeeere's Razor!'

With that I banged on the window as hard as I could – without breaking the glass. You should have seen him fucking jump. He was obviously terrified. Quick as a flash I sped off down the drive, jumped over the gate and ran home. I arrived just in time to hear the phone going. 'That'll be Alan,' I said to the ex. 'I've just put the fear of fucking God into him.' Sure enough, when I picked up the phone it was the man himself.

'RAAAAZOOOOOOOOR!' he screamed. 'THERE'S THREE GEEZAZ IN MI GARDEN, MAN. THERE'VE

GOT STOCKINGS OVER THEIR HEEDS AND EVERYTHING. THEY'RE GOING TO TRY AND NICK MA HAT-TRICK BALLS, I KNOW THEY ARE! SHALL I CALL THE POLICE?'

'No, no, no, no, no, no, no!' I said, trying to calm him down. 'Whatever you do, don't do that, son. I'll come straight up. You just stay where you are, OK? Leave it to me.'

'HURRY UP MAN!' he screamed. 'I'M TERRIFIED!'

Knowing full well that he'd be peering from behind the curtains, I grabbed a golf club as I left the house. After jumping over his gate I walked up his drive brandishing it and shouting, 'Where are yer, yer bastards? Come out and show yourselves!' I really got into character for this bit and had there been any burglars on site they'd have got a nasty shock.

When I reached the front door I could see that the letterbox was open and after bending down there were Alan's scared little eyes peering through it.

'I think they're in the trees, man,' he hissed.

'All right,' I said. 'Just you leave it to me.' I decided to take things up a level here and while Alan gazed on at his hero I started approaching his trees. 'Come down, you bastards,' I shouted while waving the club in the air. 'If you don't come down, I'll come up! I mean it. Nobody breaks into my mate's house. You upset him, you upset me. Come on, yer bastards, let's be 'avin yer!' After doing that for a few minutes I started to get bored so I went back to the letterbox and knocked at the door. A few seconds later the letterbox opened. 'I think they've gone,' I said to Alan's eyes.

'Are ya sure they're not just holding a gun t'ya heed?' he whimpered.

'No,' I said bending down to show him. 'See. I honestly don't think there's anybody there, mate.'

The letterbox then closed and after opening the door a foot or so he ushered me quickly in. After closing the door behind him Alan ran towards me, jumped up and put his arms around me like a giant Geordie koala bear. He was now fully dressed fortunately but it took me by surprise a bit, I can tell you.

'Razor, man,' he said. 'You were so brave. How can I ever thank you?'

I said, 'You'd do the same for me, wouldn't you, eh?'

'FUUUUCK OOOOOF,' he said. 'Do you think they'll come back like?'

It was time to get back into character.

'Now they've seen me, son, no chance. I think you'll be quite safe now. Don't you worry, Alan. Everything's going to be alreet. Actually, have you got any beers in? You have! Let's go to the kitchen and get one, shall we? You see, I said you should have come to the pub with me.' I was laying it on with a trowel.

After having a quick beer I got up to go home. I'd had my fun.

'Where are ya gannin' man?' he said in a panic.

'Well, I'm going home. You're all right now aren't you? *Crimewatch* has finished and the nasty men have gone.'

'Don't take the piss, man. That fukin' terrified me, that did.'

'All right,' I said. 'I'm sorry. Anyway, I'm going home now.'

'Can't yer stay?' he said as quick as a flash. 'Aww please, man.'

'No,' I said.

'Can I come and stay with you then?'

'Of course you can,' I said, patting him on the cheek and getting back into character. 'Let's go upstairs, pack you a little bag, and then we'll walk down to mine, OK?'

After packing a little bag we left the house and as we slowly walked down the drive I remained vigilant. 'What was that?' I said with a start.

'What was what?' said Alan, grabbing me by the arm.

'I could have sworn I heard something,' I said, brandishing my trusty club. After picking up the pace a bit we walked through his gate and down the road towards my place, and as we were walking up my drive I nipped ahead of him. 'Just going to warn the wife we've got a guest,' I said. 'I don't want to alarm her.' Given the circumstance I thought that was quite plausible and fortunately so did Alan.

'No worries,' he said, running towards a light.

When I got through the front door I found the wife as quick as I could and told her in ten seconds flat exactly what was going on.

'Is it OK to come in?' a voice then said from just outside the front door.

'Of course it is, mate,' I said, beckoning him inside. 'You'll be safe here, mate, I promise you.'

After making him a cup of tea we sat down for another chat. He was obviously very grateful.

'We've known each utha for a long time now, mate, and yuv aaalways been a good pal. Except for that time when yer nicked me minibar and almost finished ma career. You were a cunt then.'

'Well,' I said ignoring the bit about the minibar, 'after play-ing with you at Southampton I knew you were going to be rich one day so I thought I'd keep in with you.'

'Awwww, give awwa man! Yer takin' the piss noo!'

After he'd finished his tea I took him upstairs and showed

him his room. He stopped short of asking me to tuck him in and read him a bedtime story but I had a feeling he'd have liked one.

Once again, I thought that was now full-time on the fun but while I was getting ready for bed I had an idea.

'What are you up to now?' asked the now ex-wife.

'I've had an idea,' I said. 'I'm going to wait till he's asleep and then pay him a little visit.' With that, I grabbed my jeans, took out her tights from one of the front pockets and waved them in the air.

'Oh my God,' she said. 'He'll shit himself!'

'Let's hope he gets out of bed first!'

Now, I'm sure you'll all be very interested to know that I like to sleep in my birthday suit and after brushing my teeth I got undressed, put on the stockings and went to Alan's bedroom door. I did stop for a split second and consider what I was about to do but my conscience lost out to the thought of him crapping his pyjamas. After grabbing the door handle and muttering one-two-three, I burst into Alan's room, stood in the doorway right in front of him and shouted at the top of my voice, 'PREPARE TO DIE YOU CAAAAAAAAAAAAAAAAAAANT!'

For the second time in one night poor old Alan Shearer almost had a heart attack. I could actually see his little face and, unfortunately for him, he could see mine, covered in a black stocking. He went, 'HEEEEEEEEEEEEEEEEEELP, YER BASTAAAAAAAAAAAAAD.'

At this point my conscience actually started getting the better of me and so I decided to call it a day once and for all.

'It's OK, Alan,' I said, taking off the stockings and turning on the light. 'It's only me. Look, I'm sorry, mate,' I said. 'It was just a bit of fun.'

The look on his face went from total fear, to total confusion and then to extreme anger all in about five seconds. 'You mean it was you all along?' he said eventually.

'I'm afraid so,' I said, trying my best to appear apologetic.

'But you came up with a golf club and looked around my garden.'

'Yes, but there was nobody there,' I said. 'Only me. And you, peering through the letterbox.'

This seemed to rile Alan and as I then started giggling, which I had a feeling wouldn't help matters, Alan got out of bed very calmly, walked over to where I was standing and then bitch-slapped me. Quite hard as it goes. Shocked? You bet I was. After that he then turned me around, pushed me out of the bedroom, got dressed, packed his little bag and then went home. It took him a while to forgive me but forgive me he did. If he hadn't, I'd have haunted him. Literally!

16

The Perils of Booze

Despite being somebody who likes a drink – and who will obviously go the extra mile to have one with a mate – it doesn't always agree with me. And I don't know if you've heard this before, children, but drinking can get you in all sorts of trouble.

Take tequila, for example. I must have tried that hundreds of times over the years and every time I've tried it I projectile vomit. I'm assuming it's an allergic reaction, but I might be wrong, and the reason I keep trying it is because people keep on buying it for me and it's against my religion to turn down free drinks. The most bizarre allergic reaction I've ever heard about is Sammy Lee's. Believe it or not, he's allergic to grass, which can't have been helpful, and is why he never made sliding tackles. I used to think he was just a lazy little shit.

I nearly killed Sammy Lee one night. You see, not only do I invent great people, but I finish 'em off too. He'd just signed for Southampton and we were in a restaurant called the Loop. I'm afraid I was a bit hammered and when he asked me the way to the toilets I told him to go left instead of right. By turning left he was in danger of falling down a shaft into the cellar, which I was aware of, and because he was also three sheets to the wind that's exactly what happened. He came back about fifteen minutes later looking like someone who'd just fallen down a hole or something. To this day I've never admitted to him that I did it on purpose. Fortunately, Sammy's allergic to reading as well as grass so I think my secret's safe.

We used to go in a bar called Kingsway in Liverpool and one of the reasons we used to go in there was because all the Liverpool and Everton players used to get free booze. A bloke called Tony Adams was the manager – different one, obviously – and because we were allowed free drinks he used to let me go behind the bar and get them for all the Liverpool lads. One night, while I was behind there pouring away, this Geordie skinhead leans over from the other side and starts having a go at me. 'Aah, it's you, ya cunt,' he says. 'You broke Pete-a Beardsley's cheekbone, ya bastad! I should fuckin' do yer.' I wasn't in the mood for all that shit so I carried on pouring and told him to fuck off. 'Oh aye,' he said, standing up. 'Yer wanna gan outside, der yerz?' 'Let me get an interpreter first,' I said.

I assumed that this bloke must have been standing on the brass rail or something because he looked ridiculously tall. So, believing him to be quite small, I lost my shit and decided to take him on. 'All right then you Geordie cunt,' I said, making my way from behind the bar. 'Let have a fucking . . .'

Oh deary me. This bloke wasn't standing on the brass rail at all. He was a bona fide giant. A bona fide giant who I had just agreed to fight. Under normal circumstances a mate of mine called Gary Sandland, who was a kickboxing world champion, would have been there to get me out of trouble but he hadn't turned up yet. *What the fuck have I done?* I thought. Everybody in the bar was watching so I was just going to have to go outside and take it like a man. Or see if I could bribe him with some tickets or something.

Fortunately, as I opened the door to the bar, there was Gary walking towards me and after I bravely explained what had happened, he advised this Geordie to go back inside, have a drink and forget about it. The Geordie, who obviously wasn't a kickboxing fan, decided against this course of action and ended up getting his arse kicked. As he was lying there on the floor I walked up to him and said, 'You're lucky I didn't get hold of you!' Then, seeing an opportunity to pull the wool over everyone's eyes I ran back into the club, told everyone I'd kicked his arse from here to Newcastle and I got a massive round of applause for my trouble! Honestly, I've had more lives so far than a lorry load of cats.

Speaking of which. Lives, that is. Not cats.

I was arrested once while I was at West Ham and got put away for the night. It was during the Christmas party and I was holding the kitty, which was about four grand. I was just settling up with the landlord in one of the pubs when suddenly it kicked off and one of our lot ended up throwing a bottle at a car. It was all over in a second and while I was still paying up they all pissed off to the next boozer. As I was catching them up, a police car pulled up alongside me and, to cut a long story short, they thought I was the one who'd thrown the bottle. 'Why do you think it was me?' I asked. 'Do you have any CCTV?'

'You're wearing seventies clothes, sir, which fits the description we've been given perfectly.'

'But there's forty of us,' I said. 'And we're all wearing pretty much the same!'

For some reason, the police officer didn't believe me and I ended up getting nicked. When we got to the station the desk sergeant said, 'Could you empty your pockets please, sir?'

'Certainly,' I said, and I put the four grand on the desk.

'Where did you get that kind of money, sir?'

'It's a kitty,' I said.

'Really, sir? I doubt that very much.'

'I don't give a toss what you doubt, that four grand is a kitty for our Christmas party!'

I ended up spending a night in the cells and although they couldn't prove that I'd thrown the bottle, because I hadn't, I ended up being barred from Romford, which is where the party took place, for one week. When the magistrate passed sentence I shat my fucking pants because the West Ham training ground happens to be in Romford and I had a feeling that my manager wouldn't be too happy.

'Hello Harry,' I said after calling him up. 'I've got a bit of news.'

'Yes,' he said. 'I heard about your "news" Razor. Not guilty, wasn't it?'

'That's right, Harry. It was a case of mistaken identity.' Despite not being able to see him I knew exactly what expression he'd have on his face. It's one that says, 'Pull the other one son, it's got fucking bells on!' 'Look Harry,' I continued, 'I'm afraid I've got some bad news.'

'What is it? You fit to play at the weekend or something?'

'Worse than that, Harry. I'm banned from Romford.'

'YOU'RE WHAT?'

'I'm banned from Romford. For one week.'

'Razor, you really are a twenty-four-carat cunt! What are you?'

'A twenty-four-carat cunt.'

After each of us had confirmed the news that I was a cunt, Harry slammed the phone down and about an hour later he rang back. 'I've managed to get your sentence reduced Razor,' he said. 'But you'll have to be out of Romford by 7 p.m.'

'Not a problem, H,' I said. 'I'm usually in the bookies by three!'

17

The Hardest Men in Football

This is one of those chapters that might seem quite gratui-tous at first glance and given whose name is on the front of the book you might be forgiven for thinking that it'll be a top ten of players who liked putting the boot in. Not quite. You see, the style of football I'll be alluding to in this chapter was as much part of the game as scoring goals back in the day and the majority of players were capable of putting the boot in if they had to.

The hardest man in football for me was Jimmy Case. Being a Kevin Keegan fan, I used to watch him playing for Liverpool a lot when I was a kid and although Kevin was my hero Jimmy wasn't too far behind. The game I remember most from that period was the 1977 European Cup final against Borussia Mönchengladbach and one of the reasons I remember it, apart from Liverpool winning, of course, is because Jimmy Case murdered them. He was rumoured to have one of the hardest shots in football and in order to have the hardest shot you've got to have the hardest kick. Borussia Mönchengladbach certainly found that out!

Watching Jimmy was obviously a joy but actually getting the chance to play with him, as I did at Southampton, was dream-land. He was like a father figure in the dressing room and everyone looked up to him. Not because we were scared of him. The reason we looked up to Jimmy was because he was a great player and had medals coming out of his arse. He was also very protective of his teammates so having somebody like that looking after you used to make you feel great.

One of his nicknames at Southampton was the Silent Assassin and never has a nickname been more richly deserved. Unlike me, he never used to argue with the referee. As soon as you start arguing with a ref you're marked, but Jimmy never did that. He also used to wear a hearing aid. It was one of those old-fashioned big ones that used to loop around the top of your ear and my God did he put it to good use. During a match he'd keep it in his jockstrap and whenever there was a melee he'd carry on putting the boot in after everyone else had stopped. The referee would be blowing his whistle like a madman but he'd always carry on. Then, just before the referee reached him, Jimmy would reach into his jockstrap, pull out the hearing aid and put it on. When the referee went to reprimand him he'd lean forward with the hearing aid in full view and say, 'Oh, sorry ref. I didn't hear you.' This always used to embarrass the referees and they'd shuffle away and say, 'Oh, no problem Jimmy.'

I've seen Jimmy Case take players out with two-footed challenges that normally would have had you off and banned and these days arrested! The referee would then run over with his whistle in his mouth and start reaching for the cards and as he's doing that Jimmy would be nonchalantly reaching into his jockstrap trying to find his excuse! 'Sorry ref,' he'd say. 'I didn't hear the whistle.' I'm obviously not condoning those sorts of challenges but you have to admire his front and ingenuity. The referees would be apologising to Jimmy while the players he'd tackled were being carried off. Incredible!

We once played an away game at Everton and because he was a former Liverpool player all the crowd shouted was 'Oh, Jimmy Jimmy – Jimmy Jimmy Jimmy Jimmy shithouse Case.' This game produced a battle royal because playing up front for Everton was Graeme Sharp who, as well as having a lovely touch on him and being a great centre forward, also had in his arsenal a rather hazardous two-footed challenge. The battle came to a climax sometime during the second half when, after Jimmy had passed the ball, Sharp came in with a two-footed challenge. As it was coming in, Jimmy countered this by going over Sharp's challenge with his two feet and, after running all the way up Graeme Sharp's body, they hit him right under the chin. Afterwards he had four holes where Jimmy's boot had been and was in a right state. It was fucking brutal! The rest of the Everton players didn't even go over to Sharp. They just gestured to the bench to have him stretchered off, which he was. As all this was going on, by the way, Jimmy Case was thirty or forty yards away filling in the divots as if nothing had happened.

Make no bones about it, though, Jimmy Case could play. You just didn't mess with him. Alan Brazil always says as much on his radio show. He was a five-foot-nine Scouser and to look at him you wouldn't have thought he was capable of knocking the skin off a rice pudding. Once again, the phrase 'Never judge a book by its cover' is perfect and could have been invented for Jimmy Case.

As well as teaching me a few things on the pitch, Jimmy also taught me how to drink. What an accolade that is! Forget the four league titles, the three European Cups, the UEFA Cup and the four Charity Shields, I taught Razor Ruddock how to drink his own bodyweight in alcohol! Cheers, Jimmy.

Like it or not, that was the culture in Jimmy's day and as bizarre as it may seem now, if you didn't like a drink there's no way you would have advanced in that all-conquering Liverpool side.

At Southampton, Jimmy had obviously brought that culture with him when he joined the club and the first time I went for a drink with him he said, 'From now on, when you go for a drink you go for a drink with us. We're your new mates.' That's genuinely what it was like and although it might sound a bit menacing it was obviously an attempt at creating and building camaraderie. It was successful too. As I've said, it's much easier to play a game of football with your mates that it is your heroes or people you admire. You're also willing to go that extra mile for a mate. You'll sweat blood for them. In that respect, what Jimmy did with regards to making sure we all stuck together on the pitch and off made absolute sense and it obviously helped me as a player. It didn't help my liver much but I was young at the time and didn't care. Had he remained just a hero I'd have been too worried about upsetting him but having his friendship enabled me to advance and play to the best of my ability. Providing I didn't have a hangover, of course.

Before playing with Jimmy I'd never been that much of a drinker, believe it or not, but once he'd taken me under his wing it all changed, quite dramatically as it goes! I'm not suggesting that Jimmy Case was some kind of alcoholic, by the way. He most certainly was not. What he and others like him consumed at the bar just happened to be the rule in those days and not the exception. I was also quite a willing pupil, it has to be said, so once I got a taste for it there was no stopping me.

Not surprisingly, Jimmy Case the friend was just as committed as Jimmy Case the footballer, and when I was transfer-listed at Southampton, which was a pretty dark time for me, he was the one who kept me going. I think he could sense that I didn't have a great deal of confidence in myself as a player at the time and I genuinely feared for my future. He used to ring up and say, 'Hey, you. Don't take any notice of what those dickheads are writing in the newspapers. They know nothing. I know you're good enough and deep down you know you're good enough too. Keep going, son. Don't let the bastards grind you down!' The words themselves made a massive amount of difference but the fact they were coming from Jimmy Case made them resonate even more. This was about respect and at that time in my career I don't think I respected anybody more than Jimmy Case. Not a lot's changed really and although there are one or two people up there with him, he's still one of the best.

Another nutcase was Terry Hurlock, who I played with at Millwall. He too was five-foot-nine so he was no giant. Fuck me, was he hard though. In 2007 *The Times* rated him as the twenty-seventh hardest player in football which, believe me, is about twenty-five or twenty-sixth places out. Who the fucking hell decided that? The Archbishop of Canterbury? I once saw him beat up two bouncers at Charlie Chan's at Walthamstow dog track and he may as well have been making a cup of tea. ''Ere, you.' Bang! 'And here's one for yer mate.' Bosh! The last time I saw him he said to me, 'You see you, son. I love you that much I'd let you fuck my wife. She's got a few miles on the clock, bless her, but I'd let you have a go. That's how much I love you, Razor, and that's how much I hate her.'

When Jimmy Case left Southampton they brought Terry in as his replacement so basically it was like for like. One legendary hard nut for another. The twenty-seventh hardest man in football though? You fucking pricks.

Have we got time for another nutter? Yes, I think we have. Unlike Jimmy, this player never became a friend of mine although I did try and get to know him on several occasions. It was impossible though. Having now retired from the game I can look back and say in all honestly that he's probably the scariest player I ever came into contact with. His name was Pat Van Den Hauwe, remember him? Pat's about seven years older than me and played the majority of his football for Birmingham, Everton and Tottenham, which is where I met him. You can tell by the surname that Pat's obviously Welsh and if memory serves me correctly he was called up to the national team on several occasions. That was a joke, by the way. Pat was born in Belgium but he supposedly had a Welsh grandparent or something. Anyway, Pat was a left-back and when I joined Tottenham for the second time in 1992 he'd already been there about three years. He was the only player in the dressing room I couldn't strike up any kind of relationship with and he also had a temper like nobody I'd ever met before, and that's coming from a Millwall supporter who knew one or two people, if you see what I mean. Pat was on a different level and would explode at the slightest thing. Seriously, if he went, you made yourself scarce!

I remember watching him trying to leave the Tottenham training ground once, something that, to the majority of human beings, would have been a fairly straightforward and peaceful task. Not for Pat. It was lose it first and think later with him. There was a huge metal gate at the entrance to the training ground that opened outwards as opposed to inwards and when Pat tried pulling it one day, as opposed to trying it the other way like most people, he continued pulling it and the more it wouldn't budge the angrier he became and the angrier he became the closer the gate came to being ripped off its hinges. Because he was getting so angry nobody dared tell him that the gate opened outwards so we had to let him work it out for himself. Pat wasn't thick by the way, far from it. His temper would just take over and instead of thinking to himself, *Now because this gate won't open, I wonder if I'm doing something wrong,* he'd just go ballistic and try and remove it forcibly. After threatening to kill the gate itself, the person who designed the gate and the person who made the gate, Pat eventually got the hang of it and after slamming it shut behind him and giving it a parting kick, he got into a waiting car and hopefully took a Valium or three. We spectators just stood there agog, transfixed in a mixture of fascination and extreme fear.

Pat's nickname at the club was Reggie, as in Perrin, because as well as going ballistic on occasion he would also go missing. This would be for several days, by the way, and he'd come back offering no explanation as to where he'd been or what he'd been doing. Not that there was anybody daft enough to push him on it. We all wanted to live! I think what excused Pat's behaviour was that he was a very good player and, when he was in, a model professional. He just had his own way of dealing with life, I suppose.

You could tell what kind of mood Pat was in by his eyes. They used to speak volumes and the sooner you learned how to read them the better. It was pretty simple actually. They either said, 'I'm going to kill you,' or they said, 'I'm not going to kill you.'

When I joined the club on that second occasion I had no idea and, despite being warned about Pat's temper and him giving you the evil eye – literally – I just waded in there like a prat with a death wish. I can remember trying to crack a joke with him one day – at somebody else's else expense, by the way – and he just stared at me and said, 'Don't fucking wind me up, Razor, don't get me going!'

'Fair enough,' I said, sidling down the bench as fast as I possibly could. Those bloody eyes though!

18

That's an Absolute Shocker!

It takes a lot to shock me, and I mean a hell of a lot, either on or off the field of play. One of the most newsworthy incidents I ever witnessed was when it kicked off between Johnnie Hartson and Eyal Berkovic during that infamous training session at West Ham in 1998. Fuck me, that was an explosion and a half! I think Harry's wig almost fell off. I've seen a few clashes between teammates in my time, and I was involved in one or two, but this one was in a league of its own, pardon the pun.

It was a funny time for the team as the last two games we'd played had seen us beat Liverpool in the league, quite comprehensively, which had surprised a lot of people, and then a few days later lose to Northampton in the Worthington Cup, or the Worthless Cup as it was unfairly known (I say that as it's the only winner's medal I ever got my grubby mitts on).

The only reason it went public was because somebody – although I have no idea who – had allowed a punter into the training ground to watch the session and because he was a fan he wanted to film the occasion so brought a camcorder. It would have to be on that day, wouldn't it? Nine times out of ten a confrontation like that between two teammates would never have become public knowledge – at least back then before camera phones were about – and it would most likely have been dealt with quietly by the manager in his office.

As I said, I'd seen and had been involved in some proper training-ground scrapes over the years – good old-fashioned punch-ups – but I'd never seen anything like this before. He says, rubbing his hands with glee! I think Eyal told the newspapers back home in Israel that John had kicked his head like a football and having been standing just a few yards away when it happened I can quite categorically state that Eyal's claim wasn't too far from the truth! But it was the fact that it was caught on camera and then, once the media had got hold of it (or should I say purchased it for a massive wad of cash before slowing it down and concentrating only on the point of contact), that obviously sensationalised it. The person I felt sorry for the most was Harry. He had to try and manage the situation – sorry, debacle – and, as much as he tried to persuade the press and the public that it was a spontaneous incident and not something that had been bubbling under the surface for ages, he was fighting a losing battle. Once the press had their story, or at least the story they wanted, they ran with it, and ran, and ran, and ran. The fact that the incident happened to involve the largest player at the club seemingly trying to decapitate the smallest player at the club with his foot didn't do Mr Hartson any favours whatsoever. If it had been Razor Ruddock on the receiving end of Johnnie's size eleven then everyone would have laughed and it would still be rolled out on every *It'll Be Alright on the Night*-type show in the country, if not the world!

To be fair to John, he was full of remorse afterwards and regardless of whether they liked each other or not he would never have deliberately gone for a fellow player like that. He was fiery, and he was big, but John Hartson was no thug and had never been in the habit of trying to decapitate fellow professionals. In fact, the whole thing left him devastated, and especially when they started slowing everything down and printing photos of the moment he made contact. It's all very well the press calling out hooliganism when it happens on the terraces and what have you, but to completely sensationalise one moment of madness and turn it into something it certainly wasn't just to sell some newspapers or some adverts . . . well, you can't take the moral high ground after that, can you?

I was just a few yards away when it happened. Well, about fifty. The catalyst was a tackle that John put in on Eyal from behind and for reasons best known to him, Eyal took exception to it. As he went to the ground, Eyal threw out an arm and it just caught John, who reacted instantaneously and without thinking, as Eyal had just done, by kicking out. It looked on the footage as if John had landed a left-foot volley full-on in Eyal's face but given what I know it's my opinion that he caught him on the shoulder before flicking the side of his face. If John's boot had hit him full-on in the kisser he'd still have been in hospital and his face would have been as flat as a witch's tit. That's a fact, mate!

During our next match, the opposition had the audacity to score a goal and the players involved based their celebration on the incident. I can't remember which team it was but the scorer went down on his knees while the other pretended to kick him in the head. Had I not been involved in a similarly contentious goal celebration once – also at West Ham – with a pal of mine called Ian Wright, I'd have lambasted the players involved. The fact is, though, I haven't got a leg to stand on!

While we're here, perhaps I should remind you . . .

The only footballing incident that made more headlines than the Hartson–Berkovic debacle in 1998, although we could probably go for the entire decade with this one, was when Paolo Di Canio of Sheffield Wednesday pushed referee Paul Alcock to the ground during a game against Arsenal at Hillsborough. I could be wrong, but I don't think a player had ever pushed a referee to the ground before, certainly not during a match – that wasn't Sunday League! I still remember as clear as day watching it on TV. Despite not seeing it in the flesh like I had the other incident, this made my jaw drop like I'm sure it did everyone. And what was my reaction, you might ask? Well, I'm sorry, but I fucking well pissed myself. I'm not going to lie and say that I sat there tutting, because I didn't. It was like Cantona's kung-fu kick. I knew that was wrong in the eyes of the FA, etc., but in my eyes he'd simply done what the majority of us had wanted to do at some point during our careers. I felt a bit sorry for him. Cantona, that is, not the prick he kicked. The sardines thing that followed was a bit weird but that's Eric.

Anyway, the idea to turn Paolo's professional push on Paul into a goal celebration was obviously Ian Wright's. I don't think that will surprise anyone, as despite me liking a giggle, Wrighty was in a different league to me.

Actually, while we're here I should tell you how him and me came to be mates, because it wasn't always the case. I used to fucking hate playing against Wrighty, especially when he was playing with Mark Bright at Palace. Wright and Bright were a horrible pair. Wrighty used to come up behind me and scratch the back of my neck and when I went for him he'd shout, 'Hey, ref, what's his problem? I ain't done nothing. He just flipped!'

Once the ref had ticked me off, Wrighty would come up and say, 'Sorry about that, big'un, but your missus makes a lovely breakfast.' He used to drive me mad!

He was in the England squad when I got my first call-up and when Terry Venables read out the list of people sharing rooms I got the shock of my life. Shearer and Le Tissier were the first to be read out and then he said, 'Ruddock and Wright.' 'Oh my God,' I said. 'Please, not him!' I was at Tottenham at the time and he was at Arsenal and, as I've just suggested, we'd never been what you'd call best mates.

About ten minutes later I decided to go up to our room to dump my stuff. When I arrived the door was open. I walked in and there jumping up and down on one of the beds, stark bollock naked, was Wrighty.

'Come on then, you cunt,' he said. 'Do you want to have a go, do you? Come on then, let's 'ave yer? Come on then, you cunt. Do you want have a go, yeah? Yeah? Yeah?'

I mean, how the hell do you answer that? It really broke the ice between us and from then, once he'd covered himself up, him and me became great mates. He's probably one of the funniest people I've ever known and definitely the funniest in football. Apart from me. He was also untouchable when he was at Arsenal. Amazing player, but a pain in the fucking arse.

Anyway, when Wrighty suggested that him and me should take the piss out of Paolo and Paul, I said yes straightaway. He said, 'When I score tonight, Razor – not if – you run over to me, I'll show you a red card and then you push me over, OK?'

'Fucking hell mate, YES!' I said.

The pushing incident had only happened two days before so was still fresh in everyone's minds, especially Paolo and Paul's, bless 'em. I wonder if they were forced to make up like John and Eyal were? 'Come on Paolo, give Paul a big hug.' 'Fuck off-a! I no hug-a hiiiim.' I have a feeling they didn't.

I'm pretty sure we rehearsed the celebration once or twice beforehand and when Wrighty inevitably scored the goal, which was a late winner against my old team Southampton, it was like all our Christmases had come at once. Fortunately, I wasn't too far away when he scored and I was over there and in character in seconds. Wrighty, too, was absolutely on point and after theatrically showing me an imaginary red card I feigned Italian outrage and gave him a big pretend push. Wrighty tried his best with the fall but it was still nowhere near as theatrical as the real thing!

Him and me got pulled up in front of the FA for that, which I thought was ridiculous. You can imagine the two of us standing there, can't you? The panel from the FA were trying to be all serious and solemn but at the end of the day everyone else in the entire country seemed to find it funny, so who were we to disagree with the majority? Wrighty started giggling first and then I started, and as hard as the FA tried to make the incident into something it wasn't – and they did – it fell on deaf ears as far as we were concerned. I think we got fined about £200 each. It's a wonder they didn't give us lines.

About three months later, who joined West Ham? Yep, Paolo Di Canio. On his first day he came storming into the dressing room and said to me and Wrighty, 'Hey-a! Wadaya-think-a-you-were-doing-a-with-that-a-goal-a-celebration, eh? Everyone forget about it!' He was only joking, thank God.

Paolo ended up becoming one of the last people I ever got intoxicated against their will at a football club. It was the end of a long list! Believe it or not, he was one of the first big-name players I ever played alongside who really, really looked after themselves and as far as I know he never touched a drop of alcohol. His mantra was, 'You booze, you lose,' whereas mine was, 'Fuck off, you Italian twat, I'm having a pint.'

His fitness was incredible, though, as was his work ethic. He was always first in and last out of the dressing room and would often stay behind after training, which I found strange. As I was getting into my car I would shout, 'Oi, Paolo, the bookies are open you dickhead!'

'Piss-off-a!'

Without doubt the strangest thing about Paolo, apart from the fact that he didn't drink and stayed behind after training, was that he also used to shave his entire body. I know! I'd have to get the fucking council in to do me.

Anyway, as opposed to leaving him alone on the booze front I used to pester him like mad and one day he relented – the fool! It was curiosity that pushed him overboard. We were out on the tiles with the boys one night and somebody ordered a pint of Guinness.

'What-a the hell is that?' he asked.

'That's Guinness,' I said.

'It's-a very black!'

'Well, it's not really alcohol, you see. It's a kind of liquid food. It's healthy, too.'

'Really?' said Paolo suspiciously.

'Yep. Really. In fact, the adverts for it used to say that, "Guinness is Good for You." Why don't you try a pint?' I thought, *I've fucking got you, son.*

'Perhaps just a small glass,' he said.

'Oh no. In order for it work you have to have a pint. That's the recommended dose.'

'OK,' said Paolo. 'I try.'

I managed to get two pints down him before he realised he was pissed. It was fucking hilarious.

While we're on the subject of getting told off by the FA, which happened quite a lot when I was a player (I even had my own parking space at one point), I must tell you about the time I got done for something I said about Patrick Vieira. He'd been sent off for spitting at me at Upton Park and the week after I'd gone on *Soccer AM* as a guest.

'What was it like when he spat at you?' somebody asked, and I replied, 'He missed but I could smell the garlic on his breath.'

Vieira ended up getting a four-match suspension and a £30,000 fine for his troubles, because as well as gobbing at me he'd also sworn at a police officer in the tunnel, the naughty boy.

Arsène Wenger was not happy at all with yours truly and he even accused me of provoking Patrick. *Moi*, provoke another player? Have a day off. He said, 'We have to ensure that the provocateurs are judged in the same light as the people they provoke. For me, what Ruddock said after the game was more shocking even than what he did on the field.' Never mind about Patrick Vieira spitting at somebody and swearing at a police officer, Razor Ruddock said that Patrick's breath smell of garlic! What a load of bollocks.

I ended up getting hauled before the FA on a misconduct charge and I had to hire a flaming barrister. He was good, though, and when the FA asked me why I'd claimed that his breath had smelt of garlic I was ready for them. 'Because it did,'

I said. That stumped them. Apparently when the FA had asked Patrick why he'd spat at me he'd said, 'Because he called me a French prat.'

'Is this true?' asked a member of the panel.

'Absolutely not, sir,' I said. 'The word prat is not part of my vocabulary.'

Fortunately, he didn't press me for what I actually called him, which is just as well as it certainly wasn't prat. I ended up getting off on that one, which made a nice change.

The most ridiculous fine I ever got from the FA was when I was playing for Palace in 2000–1. A lot of players were starting to have either their first names or their nicknames put on the back of their shirts as opposed to their surname and, never one to be outdone in the football fashion stakes, I decided to have a word with the kit man and ask him to have Razor put on mine. After one game some dickhead complained and I was hauled up in front of the FA and handed a £75 fine. I dread to think how much it cost the FA to fine me £75. Thousands, probably. And all because I had my nickname put on my shirt. They could have called up the club and told them to tell me not to do it again but that would have been far too straightforward.

One of the biggest shocks I ever had away from the pitch, but still in my capacity as a footballer, happened when Spurs were playing Real Zaragoza away during my second spell there. After the game, we all went out on the piss and when I got back to my hotel room my bed wasn't there. I must have gone out of my room and come back in again about ten times as I just couldn't believe it had happened. I was also too scared to go down to reception and report it missing. I thought they'd lock me away! After pacing up and down inside my room for an hour or so I looked out of the window by chance and there in the middle of the car park was my bloody bed. Once again, I had to look away from the window and look back again about ten times before I believed it was real. The first thought that came to me when I did was, *How the fucking hell am I going to explain this?* Without an excuse I just had to come clean and say that it had mysteriously disappeared but nobody believed me. Terry Venables went absolutely mental when he found out and made me pay for a new one. The perpetrators, by the way, which I found out the following day, were Vinny Samways and Andy Gray. They just did it for lolz, apparently. There, I've named and shamed you, you pair of dickheads!

You owe me a fucking bed.

19

The Name's Ruddock, Razor Ruddock

One of the most popular stories I tell when I do my after-dinner speeches is the one involving Sean Connery. I say that as if you'll know which one I'm talking about but it's such a well-told tale that some of you probably will. Even so, for the benefit of those who haven't heard it, I'm going to give it an airing here but even if you have heard it I advise you to read on as I'm not pushed for time like I usually am. Anyway, I'd grab yourself a can for this one.

When I was at West Ham we used to go and play golf at Wentworth occasionally. The only reason they let the likes of us play there was because we were pro-footballers, and I'm pretty sure this gave a lot of the older members the right hump. In fact, I know it did, because I remember the looks they used to give us after we'd had a few. To make matters worse, we used to take Wrighty with us when we went to Wentworth and, as somebody who doesn't play golf, has no idea of the etiquette involved and doesn't care – and has no filter when it comes to opening his mouth – he was your average golf snob's worst bloody nightmare. That never used to bother us, though, and it certainly never bothered him. Wrighty's a professional wind-up merchant and it was always fertile hunting ground for him. He was also an excellent beer monitor and took his role very seriously.

On this particular day, the beer in question was Stella – that's the old Stella, not the new weaker stuff – and after finishing the round of golf we ensconced ourselves in the bar, ordered a massive plate of ham, egg and chips each and started washing it all down with a few pints of the aforementioned loopy juice. After six or seven pints we were all well over halfway there and Wrighty in particular was becoming quite animated. He's hyperactive at the best of times but after half-a-dozen vintage Stellas he'd become even more unpredictable.

At the back of the bar at Wentworth there's a big conservatory bar and, while the rest of us were sitting around a table becoming more and more incoherent, Wrighty was hopping around looking for someone to annoy. Suddenly I heard him gasp and after running over to our table he told us all to shut up.

'Fuuuuuucking hell, lads,' he said. 'You'll never guess who's just walked in to the bar over there. It's only James Bond!'

'Fuuuuuck ooooof,' I said. 'You're pissed.'

Instead of arguing Wrighty just pointed over to the conservatory bar and there, standing at the bar having obviously just finished a round of golf together were Jimmy Tarbuck, Bruce Forsyth, God bless him, and Sean Connery. Wrighty was right!

Had we all been sober we may well have asked all three of them for an autograph, but we weren't. We were pissed.

'Excuse me, waiter,' said Wrighty, beckoning one over. 'You see that man at the bar with the grey hair and the beard. The one standing next to the man with the wig. Yeah, that's him. I want you to take him a vodka Martini, shaken not stirred.'

Because of the state we were all in we thought this was the funniest thing that had ever happened in the history of the universe. As the waiter went away to do Wrighty's bidding we all huddled around the table and started giggling our arses off. We were like schoolkids.

The reaction from Mr Connery when his drink arrived was not what we'd been hoping for. We thought he'd see the funny side but when the waiter pointed over to our table while obviously divulging the origin of the drink, he gave us a look that said just one thing really. 'Fuck right off!' As opposed to sobering our mood a bit this just made us worse and as Bond, Brucie and Tarby stood there giving us daggers, our giggles turned into guffaws and the guffaws into shrieks. They weren't happy.

Before we left for the day, Harry Redknapp had taken me to one side. 'Don't make tits of yourselves, Razor,' he'd said. 'Just behave yourselves, OK. You're in charge.'

As we all sat there wetting ourselves this conversation kept on replaying in my head and, although it didn't stop me laughing, I did think about trying to make amends. I knew Tarby from my Liverpool days so decided that the best thing to do would be to go over and apologise on behalf of all of us and offer to buy them a drink – of their choice!

I felt like the condemned man walking towards the conservatory but after saying hello to Tarby, introducing myself to the other two and then apologising to Sean, they seemed to mellow slightly. Just then, Wrighty popped up next to me and before I could say anything he went to shake Bruce's hand.

'Have a good game did we, my love?' he said, sticking out his chin. 'Good game, good game, good game. Have a look at the old scoreboard!'

After that he started pissing himself laughing and as I stood there gobstruck he ran off back to the table where the rest of the lads were in hysterics – again. There was no point me trying to make excuses or apologise so I just nodded at the three of them and then hightailed it.

'Bloody hell Wrighty,' I said, trying to be all sensible. I find it difficult to get angry with Wrighty at the best of times but after seven or eight pints it's impossible. 'You're a fucking nutcase,' I said, tucking into a new pint.

About twenty minutes later I heard somebody say, 'Tara lads,' and when I looked up Tarby and Brucie were leaving the bar.

'Good game, Bruce!' shouted Wrighty as a parting gift.

'Fucking shut up,' I said punching him in the nuts. 'Leave the man alone!' It was all getting a bit raucous now.

A few minutes later I looked over at Mr Connery and all of a sudden I was engulfed by a swathe of admiration. It must have been the Stella, I suppose, which is strange really as after ten pints of Stella, which is probably what we'd had by this point, I'd usually start hating everyone's guts. I must have been over-whelmed by his legendary status. And let's be honest, as legends go they don't come much bigger than him.

Just as I was mid-gaze, thinking about what it must be like having Sean Connery as a mate and wondering if I should go over there and offer him a drink, one of the lads tapped me on the shoulder. They must have been aware of the fact that the Stella was making me admiring of Mr Connery and they were keen to put things right.

'Go and knock him out,' they said.

'Who?'

'Sean Connery.'

'Why?'

'He's mugging you off, Raze,' he said.

'What the fucking hell do you mean, he's mugging me off? Have a day off will ya?'

'When we came in, everyone wanted your autograph, and when he came in, everyone wanted his instead. I'm telling you, Raze, Sean Connery's mugging you off, mate. Go and knock him out.'

'Fuck off, knobhead!' I said.

'Don't you tell me to fuck off!'

A typical Stella situation was now developing but instead of knocking it on the head we carried on drinking, and the more we drank, the angrier we became. Not just with each other, but with ourselves! Just then Wrighty came over and gave me a dead arm.

'Are you really prepared to let an actor mug you off in front of your mates?' he said. 'Go and knock him out, Raze. Go on!'

Stella Artois – as was – was the only beer or lager I've ever known that could make you turn with just another mouthful. With most beers it's another pint. As Wrighty and the others carried on goading me I remember taking a swig from my glass and after swallowing it something inside me just clicked. It was like Jekyll and Hyde. 'Is he mugging me off?' I said, sitting up. 'He is, isn't he, he's mugging me off. I'm going to knock that cunt out!' As far as the lads were concerned this was a victory and as I became angrier the goading continued. 'I fucking am, I'm going to knock him out.'

'So you should, Raze. So you fucking should.'

After continuing to talk shite for God knows how long the waiting was finally over and after standing up and downing my pint I marched over the conservatory and stopped about five yards from my target.

'Oi, Connery,' I shouted, 'I bet you've fucked some famous birds intcha? Anyone I should know about before I knock you fucking out?' I don't know where that line came from but it seemed like a good idea at the time.

Stella and testosterone notwithstanding, when Mr Connery turned around and looked at me I sobered up in about two seconds flat. He was absolutely fucking fuming! 'Oh shit,' I said to Wrighty, who'd marched up behind me. 'What the hell am I going to do?'

'Well,' he said, 'if he comes over you're going to have to knock him out as planned. You've told your mates you're going to do it.'

'But I don't think I can now. Look at his stare!' Just then he started walking over to us and as he did I grabbed Wrighty's arm. 'Fuuuucking hell, mate. What am I going to do?' Fortunately, he stopped about a couple of yards from us and when he did he gave me exactly the kind of stare I get from my missus when I come in late. Like a day late! 'Wrighty,' I said, 'I need to go to the loo!'

The stare seemed to last forever and it took every drop of willpower not to run over and plead for his forgiveness. Then, once he knew that his stare had had its effect, he turned around and walked out. The only word I can think of that describes how I felt at that moment is humiliated. I felt two inches tall. Wrighty didn't. He'd come around and was now back in goading mode. 'Why did you ask him what famous birds he'd shagged, you dickhead? Go out into the car park and knock him out. Go on, go on, go on.' The annoying little shit!

As me and Wrighty were arguing about whether or not I was going to go out to the car park and punch Sean Connery, the man himself walked back into the bar again. 'Razor, he's coming back!' squealed Wrighty, grabbing my arm. I had my back to him at the time and as Wrighty clung on to my arm I froze. Suddenly, there was a tap on my shoulder.

'Razor,' said a very familiar voice.

'Y-y-y-yes, Mr Connery,' I said, turning around.

'Zsa Zsa Gabor, in the rough, 1963.'

By this time, the rest of the lads were standing with us and the moment he said it the lot of us just broke into absolute hysterics. Whether it's true or not I obviously couldn't say but what a fucking line!

20

Not Tonight, Razor

In 1987, while I was at Spurs, we went on a pre-season tour to Norway, as you do. Why they chose Norway I have no idea but they were all there – Hoddle, Waddle, Ardiles, Clemence. I was still only a kid so to be effectively going on holiday with a bunch of living legends was pretty special.

Unfortunately, we lost the first game, which was in Oslo, and after getting back to the hotel the manager, David Pleat, who'd arrived at the club shortly after me the year before, issued our orders for the evening. 'I don't mind you going for a few drinks, lads,' he said, 'providing you're over nineteen. Those who aren't will have to stay in.'

I thought, *You wanker!* I was the only player on the tour who was under nineteen, which meant I had to stay in all night on my own. We were supposed to be a team, for heaven's sake. And we were supposed to do everything together. Well, almost everything. Certainly having a drink!

As you'd expect, instead of commiserating with me the rest of the lads laid it on with a trowel and I think each and every one of them made a point of knocking on my door as they were leaving the hotel. 'See you later, Raze,' they said. 'Hope you can find some decent porn. Channel 86 is good!'

At about half past eight I was staring out of my hotel window wondering what they were all getting up to when suddenly I saw David Pleat and one of the coaches walking into the hotel. I could have been wrong but I was pretty sure they'd been out for something to eat so the chances are they wouldn't be going out again. *Fuck it*, I thought, *I'm going out to find the lads!*

I'm not sure if Mr Pleat had ostracised me on purpose but it felt like he had. Because I'd arrived at the club before him I wasn't his signing and I think that irked him a bit. I don't think he liked me as a person either, which is fair enough. To some people, I was like Marmite in those days. Fucking horrible! It was disappointing being left out, but it wasn't a surprise.

Anyway, after throwing my glad rags on I headed off into town. The lads had told me where they were going to be, just in case I got a reprieve, and I was there within about ten minutes. The reception they gave me was hilarious. They obviously knew I'd sneaked out without Pleat's permission and acted accordingly. 'RAZOOOOOOOOOOOOOOOOR,' they all shouted. 'He's gonna fucking kill you if he finds out!' Everyone was obviously quite merry and so we all started dancing about and cheering.

'Get us a fucking drink somebody,' I shouted. One of the lads then passed me a pint and after taking a massive swig I spun around, stumbled a bit and went straight into David bloody Pleat. Fortunately, I didn't do him an injury but he obviously wasn't happy.

'I saw you watching me from your hotel window, Razor,' he said. 'So I set you a trap. I knew you'd come out. And you know what I'm going to do with you? I'm going to get rid of you.'

If I'd had to pick the worst thing that could have happened to me at that moment, apart from my family or friends coming to harm and World War III starting, it would have been losing my job at Spurs, so I literally went from having the lot and being the happiest man on earth to losing everything and being on my arse in a split second. The first thing that came into my head was my dad. He and my mum were living in Saudi Arabia at the time where he was working and if Pleat followed through with his threat, my dad would probably have to come back over to the UK. That, as a scenario, scared the living shit out of me so it's safe to say that the day was becoming a bit of a stinker.

After frogmarching me back to the hotel without saying a word, Mr Pleat deposited me outside my room, reminded me what time we were due in reception to catch the coach, said goodnight and then buggered off. I went straight to bed. I felt physically sick and could hardly move. As far as I was concerned my career had come to an end. No other clubs would have me and my parents, apart from being very angry and disappointed, would probably never speak to me again. This was all in my head, of course, but at the time it felt very, very real and I didn't get a wink of sleep. Not a single minute. I remember looking at my watch and as the hours ticked by I became more and more tired, but instead of sleeping I just lay there worrying.

I think we had to meet in reception at about 10 a.m. but instead of going down for breakfast I just stayed in bed. I wasn't looking forward to seeing anybody, least of all Pleat, so the longer I could avoid them the better. The only consolation at this point was that Pleat wouldn't have been able to contact my parents yet so the final nail in my coffin couldn't yet be hammered in.

When I dragged myself out of the lift I saw Ossie, Glenn and a few of the other lads sitting on some sofas in the middle of the reception area. I couldn't keep on avoiding everyone so decided to go and sit with them. When they saw me walking towards them they all started cheering.

'You lucky bastard!' one of them said. 'Talk about good timing.'

I almost couldn't be bothered to ask what they were on about but I decided to go along with it.

'What are you talking about?' I said, trying not to sound too depressed.

'Pleat's gone,' said Glenn.

'Eh?! You're joking.'

'I'm not,' he said smiling. 'He's resigned.'

Once again, the first person who came into my head was my old man, except instead of flying over from Saudi Arabia, kicking me up the arse and making my life a misery like he had been doing in my head the night before, he was now staying where he was. Unless David Pleat decided to call him anyway, which was unlikely as he'd had to resign for something quite embarrassing (according to the papers he had a fondness for ladies of the night) and probably wouldn't be contacting anyone in the near future, Dad would never find out. I was in the clear.

Thank you, Mr Pleat. That was quite a gesture!

This reminds me of a similar story, except instead of me getting it in the neck, a few of us did, including Mr Roy Evans.

When Gérard Houllier first came to Liverpool in 1998 he was joint manager with Roy Evans. Even so, you could tell that it was Gérard calling the shots from day one and he started making his presence felt during the pre-season tour of

Scandinavia. On the first day, just as we were all arranging where we were going to go on the piss, Gérard pops up and says, 'No going out tonight, boys. I want you all in bed early and ready for training tomorrow.' Because he was new and a bit of an unknown quantity, nobody dared say anything but we exchanged a few nods as if to say, 'He can fuck right off!'

After dinner, I got hold of a few of the lads and said, 'Reception in an hour, OK boys, pass it on,' and went up to put my glad rags on. An hour later me and Jamie Redknapp left our room and jumped into the lift but as the door opens on the ground floor there's Gérard Hool-a-Hoop. Oh bollocks! After getting out of the lift he started having a right go at us.

'Zee English mentality is all wrong,' he said. 'You are only interested in getting drunk!'

'Not *just* getting drunk,' said Jamie under his breath.

Just then the lift went 'ping' and when the door opened there was Roy Evans with his fucking dancing gear on! Hool-a-Hoop went mental and from then on their relationship was doomed to failure.

Funnily enough, I left the club after that tour. Poor old Roy, though. When we were on tour or playing in Europe we used to buy loads of women's underwear and put it in his luggage on the way back so when he got home his wife would go, ''Ere Roy, what the fuck's this?' He used to come running in the next day. 'You fucking dickheads!' he'd say. 'It took me two hours to explain about that underwear!'

21

Managers Ruled My Life

People who aren't involved in the game of football often don't realise how much influence a manager can have on the life of a footballer. I'm talking about life in general, by the way, so on the pitch and off. The first time this became apparent to me was when I started playing silly buggers at Millwall. George Graham was a formidable man who demanded good behaviour and on the one or two occasions when I stepped out of line I realised that, if he saw fit, he could change my life forever. The same thing happened when David Pleat caught me out on the piss with the lads at Tottenham. Had he not resigned the day after then he would have been at liberty to bugger up my entire career and the chances are I would have ended up doing something else. What I'm trying to get across is that these managers had a massive amount of power in those days and, as you'd expect, they didn't always use it wisely. These days that power has been diluted somewhat and I'm not sure whether that's a good thing or a bad thing. Probably a bit of both.

When I started at Millwall I was on £24.50 as an apprentice. Then it went up to £120 a week, which was amazing. I felt like a king! Honestly, I wanted to stay at that club forever. I had money and I was doing my dream job at my favourite club. Then, George Graham said he wanted to sell me. Actually, that's not quite the truth because George was forced to sell me. He had to call my dad in Saudi Arabia first but once he'd got the go ahead he contacted Spurs, who had shown an interest.

Because my dad was out of the country George was kind of responsible for me in a way, so when it came to negotiating my contract, etc., he came with me. In hindsight, had my old man been in the country I'd have told him to stay at home because George obviously knew exactly how to play these people and he was almost as good a negotiator as he was a manager.

After walking into the office at Spurs they immediately offered me £240 a week. My gob hit the floor – £240 a week! That was a fortune in my book and I was ready to sign on the line. Suddenly, before I could tell them how much I loved them – and I did love them at the time – George piped up.

'Two-forty a week?' he sneered. 'You've brought us all this way to offer him two-forty a week? That's an insult. Come on, Neil,' he said grabbing me by the arm. 'We're leaving!'

I was like a kid being dragged out of a free sweetshop without having filled my bag. 'Yes, but don't you think that's a good offer?' I said, trying to slow him down.

'No I do not, Neil. I think that's a dire offer. Come on, we're going back to the Den.'

About a second after leaving the office (George left the door open, obviously for a reason) one of the Spurs people called us back in.

'Hang on,' they shouted. 'How about two-eighty?'

'Not interested,' said George.

By now I was starting to sweat a bit. I might not have had much experience in negotiation but I had a feeling that this person was about to tell us to fuck off. I was wrong!

'OK then,' he said. 'Final offer. Three-twenty a week and a brand new Ford XR2.'

'YES!' I shouted. George shot me a look as if to say, 'Who gave you permission to speak?' I shot him one back that said, 'Please can I fucking sign?' This was all my birthdays and all my Christmases come at once for at least the next three hundred years.

When the XR2 arrived I was in seventh heaven. It even had a red go-faster stripe down the side! My favourite band at the time were Kool & the Gang (yes, I know!) and I'll tell you how advanced and fucking posh this car was: when I put my Kool & the Gang tape into the car stereo and pressed fast forward, it stopped at the next song! You didn't have to guess. Fucking beat that, mate.

When Terry Venables came into Tottenham after Pleat it was like a breath of fresh air but then after about a year he decided to sell me. 'Go somewhere else and learn your trade and I'll buy you back,' he said. 'I promise.'

I was absolutely gutted at the time because I was so happy where I was but without him making that decision for me then I may never have progressed. Portsmouth came in for me and then Southampton, and I ended up going there. Three years later, true to his word, Terry bought me back for £750,000 and made me captain. What a manager though. As good as the majority of the other managers I played for were, I learned more from Terry Venables than the rest of them put together, partly because he was just such a great manager, but also because I hung on his every word, and they weren't all compliments, believe me!

When I was captain we played Arsenal away once and by half time we were 3–0 up. I was absolutely magnificent that day, or so I thought, and they hadn't had a kick. When I walked into the dressing room I was covered head to toe in mud and I felt like a fucking hero. *Spurs are 3–0 up at Highbury at half time and you're the fucking captain? Have some of that!* I'd been into absolutely everything and when Terry Venables walked into the dressing room I was expecting nothing less than a big pat on the back and a string of well-chosen tributes. As you've probably guessed by now, I was in for a shock.

'Look at the state of you,' he said. 'You useless piece of shit!' He was bright red and spitting fucking feathers.

'What?' I said, picking my chin up off the floor. I was completely gobstruck.

'To think your dad's come all the way from Saudi Arabia to watch you play like that. You're a disgrace. And look at the state of you. You've heard of Bobby Moore, I suppose?'

'Yeah, of course I have.'

'He never got as dirty as that, and do you know why? Because he was always in the right position. You, on the other hand, are always in the wrong position which is why you look like a fucking rugby player.'

Then, he walked over to a player who I thought had been absolutely rubbish and said well done. *Right then*, I thought. *I'm going to show you!* In the second half I really did play well – it wasn't just in my head – and as I was walking off I saw Terry and I thought, *You clever fucker.* He'd known exactly what he was doing and it had worked like a dream.

He was able to build a team, create a wonderful sense of camaraderie and treat every player as an individual all at the same time. That takes some fucking doing, in my opinion. Talk about spinning plates! The thing is, it wasn't just the players who Terry Venables used to treat as individuals, it was our families too. He used to walk into the players' lounge after a game and there'd be all the players and all their mums and dads and what have you. There'd be people everywhere. When Terry walked in, he'd go over and say hello to each and every one of these family members and, providing he'd already met them, he'd remember every single one of their names. He'd walk straight up to my mum and say, 'Hello Joyce,' as if she was an old family friend. 'Where's Ted then? Oh, there he is, I can see him. Let me go and say hello to him.' My mum would come running up to me after that and say, 'Did you see that? Terry's just come up to say hello to me! What a lovely man he is.' It was the same with my kids and my brothers. Every member of my immediate family was on first-name terms with Terry Venables and that was an amazing feeling for all of us. You know what they say: happy family, happy footballer.

It was only after I retired that I fully appreciated what a genius that man was. His approach to the game was obviously complex and covered every single angle yet at the same time it was seamless. As I said, building a team while treating every player individually can't have been easy but Terry Venables made it look like a doddle.

Unfortunately, he then left after about a year and shortly after that I fell out with the chairman, Alan Sugar. At the time I couldn't stand the bloke but I respect what he did for Tottenham and what he did for other people's careers.

When Mr Sugar put me up for sale I had Brian Clough at Forest, Kenny Dalglish at Blackburn, Walter Smith at Rangers, Glenn Hoddle at Chelsea, Kevin Keegan at Newcastle and

Graeme Souness at Liverpool all after me. Even though I already had a good idea which team I wanted to join, which was Liverpool, out of respect I promised that I would speak to every single manager. I spoke to Kenny Dalglish on the Monday. That was on the phone, and then later on I saw his assistant Ray Harford in person. On the Tuesday I went to Anfield to meet Graeme Souness. He met me at the door and didn't say a word. He just grabbed me by the arm and walked me through the stadium. After making made me touch the 'This is Anfield' sign he then walked me on to the pitch, led me to the centre circle and said, 'Can you imagine playing here?' I didn't say as much but I thought, *Yeah, that's it. I'm coming here.*

One of the other reasons I signed for the club was because always I used to hate playing against Liverpool. I remember going there with Southampton when I was eighteen or nineteen and while we were warming up before the match I called over to Jimmy Case. ''Ere, Jimmy,' I said, 'when we get a corner is it two hands far post?'

He said, 'Let's just get a corner first son, OK? We'll worry about that later.'

I think we got beat about 5–0 and we didn't get one corner.

Souness was a hard fucker. Sorry, *is* a hard fucker. In training on a Friday, if you were in Souness's team you knew you'd be playing the next day because if you weren't in his team and you played in a position that was conflicted he'd two-foot you. He'd just put you out for a week so he didn't have to drop you. It normally happened to Don Hutchinson, so if he was in Souness's team he'd be full of it and if he wasn't he'd be, well, a little bit sheepish! He wouldn't try and kill him. He'd just put him out for a few days.

In training, Souness was still easily the best player. I've never, ever seen commitment like it. I remember playing in Paul Miller's testimonial match at Tottenham. It was 1986 and the visiting team were Rangers with whom Souness was player-manager. During the game I kicked somebody (by mistake) and he came charging over and squared up to me. I was only eighteen and I don't mind admitting that I absolutely shat myself. Then, when he signed me for Liverpool, I reminded him of that and said something along the lines of, 'You wouldn't square up to me now, would you, gaffer?'

'Yes I fucking would,' he said, and he was being serious! It was time to shit myself again.

'Just having a laugh, gaffer,' I said quickly.

I fucking love Souness. What a player and what a man. If you ever meet him, for fuck's sake don't use your wanking arm to shake hands. You'll be ruined!

I must give an honourable mention to Sir Alex Ferguson here, as although he never had the pleasure of managing me he did scare the shit out of me once or twice. The first time was after a game at Old Trafford. During the match I'd smashed Mark Hughes to pieces and afterwards I saw Sir Alex walking towards me. *Oh shit*, I thought. *I'm in for it now!*

It was towards the end of my Liverpool career so I'd lost a bit of pace but when I saw him walking towards me I was like an albino Usain Bolt! I actually cowered behind a coach until he'd walked past. I was that scared! Many years later I was at Lord's Cricket Ground and I saw him again. This time, though, there was no hiding place and as our eyes eventually met a look of recognition began to invade his happy, smiling face.

'That's it,' he said as he walked past me, 'the dirty bastard with the left foot.'

'That's the one,' I said, before breaking into a trot and making myself scarce.

22

Everyone Likes a Flutter!

One thing I love is a day out at the races and over the years I've had more than my fair share of luck. I don't win them all, of course, but when I do it tends to be quite big. The best example I can think of is when me and some of the Liverpool lads won a tidy fourteen grand each at the Cheltenham Festival. What a day that was! There was twelve of us and after each putting in £500 we split up and put it all on three horses, Blowing Wind, one I can't remember and Unsinkable Boxer. When the first two came in we were obviously a bit excited but when Unsinkable Boxer came up the hill in the lead and romped home at lovely to one, we went wild. My hat went straightaway and I must have kissed about two hundred people.

Once the initial euphoria had died down one of the lads said, 'Fucking hell, boys. What are we going to tell our other halves?'

Without even having to be asked we got into a huddle and began working out our story. 'Give 'em a monkey each,' I suggested, 'and we'll keep the rest at the training ground.' We knew the cash would go back to the bookies eventually so it made sense.

All our bets had gone on the Tote and when we went to collect the winnings the woman behind the counter had us all in stitches. 'Can we pay you by cheque?' she said.

'Have a day off,' I said. 'Absolutely no chance!'

'But it'll take us at least two hours to get the cash.'

'We'll be fucking here, don't you worry yourself. We ain't going nowhere!'

We ended up buying a horse with some of the proceeds. Or at least some of us did. Six of us put £1,500 in, which bought the horse and paid for it for a year. Michael Meagher from Skelmersdale was the trainer and we even got to choose the horse. For that, we had to go over to Ireland for a couple of days, which was a bind, and we ended up choosing our horse on the basis that it was by far the most violent one we'd seen. All it did was kick and bite the other horses so we thought, *You'll do for us.*

After that, we had to name it. The first one we applied for was Betty Swollocks, followed by Mary Hinge and then Keef Burtains, but all three were rejected. No sense of humour, these people.

In the end, Robbie Fowler suggested we call it Some Horse. He said, 'Can you imagine the commentator going, "And here's Some Horse coming up on the inside." It'll be hilarious.'

While I think hilarious was probably stretching it a bit, we'd given up trying to get away with something rude so that's what we went for.

Some Horse's first race was at Haydock Park and the way she came out of the stalls wasn't too dissimilar to the way I used to come out of the dressing room after a difficult first half in February. Even so, she still ended up finishing second and we all thought, *Hello, we might have something here.* Her next race was at Pontefract but Michael Meagher told us not to bother. 'She doesn't stand a chance,' he said.

Despite that, we still turned up and on the course you could get anything from 55–1 to 100–1 on her. Because of what Michael had said we ended up whacking on £250 each way just for a laugh but used the bookie offering 55–1 as the one offering 100–1 was up the other end. It wouldn't make any difference, we thought, as she was a no-hoper. Well, she only bloody won! We were obviously elated but then realised that had we not listened to Michael – her bleeding trainer – we could have got 100–1! I ended up buying a garden shed and paying off my mum's car with the winnings.

Some Horse ran seven times and won three before we had to retire her with a bad back. I decided to quit while I was ahead but Robbie Fowler and Michael Owen got well into it after that and it's become a way of life to them. Not me. I know when I've had a good run!

My wagers away from the race track haven't always been as profitable. One that springs to mind cost me almost double what I won at Cheltenham. I was playing for West Ham at the time and me and a few of the lads had decided to go Langan's Brasserie on Piccadilly, which at the time was owned by Michael Caine. After sinking several bottles of wine – each – some fat dickhead called Ruddock piped up and suggested that we all have a game of spoof. This went OK for a few minutes until I piped up again and said something along the lines of, 'I'll tell you what, lads, whoever loses the next game has to go straight out to the nearest dealership and buy a brand new Jaguar.' I also suggested that whoever didn't lose would be able to choose the colour and the trim.

I don't have to tell you what happened next, do I?

What a fucking knobhead.

I'm not known for thinking before I speak and when my mouth gets me into trouble it's usually because I've called some-body a cunt – or worse. It's funny but the moment I opened my mouth I knew it was going to end badly and when it turned out I'd lost, the table went into fucking meltdown.

''Ere, mate,' shouted one of my fellow players to a passing waiter. 'Where's the nearest Jaguar dealership?'

I forget where it was now but, after paying the bill (fortu-nately, I was excused on account of what was about to happen), I was frogmarched by the others to the nearest dealership where I would soon become the proud owner of a brand new Jaguar. It wasn't so much having to buy a car that bothered me (although it fucking well did when I came to sell it!), it was the fact that a bunch of pissed-up idiot footballers would be choosing it. I'm not sure why, but we footballers are often accused of lacking taste so you'd think there'd be a possibility that when asked to be deliberately gaudy the opposite might occur. Not a fucking chance!

These boys knew exactly what they were doing. The only person I can think of who would have wanted to take this thing for a spin is Austin Powers. The colour they chose was bright purple and it had yellow dials and beige seats with bright green piping. It was fucking gross, I tell you. Gross! The cost of my new purple Shaguar was a cool £62,000 and when I finally managed to get rid of the bloody thing about a month later, to somebody who must have been either colour-blind or a foot-baller with even less taste than the average one, I'd lost twenty-four grand. My ex-wife went absolutely batty, not surprisingly.

While we're on the subject of West Ham, which we kind of were, Harry Redknapp once came out with an absolute blinder.

We were up north playing either Leeds or one of the Sheffield teams in the quarter-final of the FA Cup and before the match he got up to give us his team talk. After telling us all to shut the fuck up he said, 'Right then you lot. It's really important that West Ham win the FA Cup this year, because if we win the FA Cup I'll get loads of money to spend and I'll be able to buy some better players for next season. Right then, off you go, lads. Do your best.'

That was his bloody team talk! We all pissed ourselves laughing. Whether it was out of spite or not I don't know, but we ended up getting beat.

While we're on the subject of the venerable Mr Redknapp . . .

23

Call Me Harry!

Harry Redknapp was the only manager I ever played for who preferred being called by his first name. It's not that all the managers I played for insisted on being called gaffer or boss, but unless they stipulated that they'd like you to call them something else you nearly always went with one of the two. Not Harry though. You'd say, ''Ere boss,' and he'd say, 'Don't be a cunt, son, I'm 'arry.'

I've got hundreds of stories about this great man and one or two are already included elsewhere in the book. My favourite though is the time when he and I went into battle over a fine he gave me. He tells this story when he does his talks and I tell it when I do mine but as I said before, you always miss some of the detail when you're telling it live so I'm going to give you the full nine yards.

Towards the end of the 1999–2000 season I got injured. When that happened you had to get yourself signed off by the physio or the doctor but you still had to come into training every day until you were fit, even after the season had finished. Unfortunately for me I was still injured after the final game, which presented a bit of a problem. Incidentally, I was playing for West Ham away at Wimbledon once and during the first half I banged heads with Carl Leaburn and fractured my eye socket. I went in at half time and after questioning my masculinity and my parentage, Harry sent me out for the second half and made me play the full ninety minutes. I was out for three weeks after that!

Anyway, back then, once the season had finished, Alan Shearer, Jim Davidson, Stephen Hendry and me would always fly up to Gleneagles for a couple of days and have some fun. We used to take our other halves with us and for a time it became a bit of a ritual. This year, because I was still injured, I was supposed to report to the physio every day, which meant no trip. After weighing things up I decided to do the decent thing and ring in and say that I had the flu. The following day me and my ex-wife were on a plane to Scotland with Alan, Stephen and their wives. Jim Davidson was running late and turned up that night with a model friend of his who, for the sake of this story, will have to remain unnamed.

'Where you two been then?' I asked him when they turned up.

'Don't you talk to me about where we've been,' said Jim. 'We've been to New York, ain't we.'

As Jim's talking this model's going, 'For God's sake, don't tell him, Jim. It's private!'

'I don't care,' he said. 'Razor, she's had her fanny lips clipped.'

'You what?'

'It's true. Her fanny was like a lettuce so we went to New York and had some of the leaves taken off. Now you know where they got the roof for the Millennium Dome!'

Even the model had to laugh at this. I was on the bloody floor!

As well as the aforementioned three mates and their respective other halves, Mike Newell and his missus were also joining us at Gleneagles and unfortunately he and I ended up having a fight on the first night. It was about something and nothing really but because it was fisticuffs it ended up making it into the papers.

Harry Redknapp might prefer the racing pages to the football ones but there was no escaping the argy-bargy between me and Mike, and when Harry found out what had happened he fined me a week's wages. The only way you could appeal a fine like this was if the letter informing you about it failed to arrive within fourteen days and this one arrived on the fifteenth, so I decided to appeal.

'What are you appealing for, Raze?' said Harry. 'You were done bang to rights, son, you don't stand a cat in hell's chance.'

'Nah, your letter arrived late, Harry. I ain't giving up a week's wages if I don't have to.'

It ended up becoming two weeks' wages as I was done for fighting *and* for skiving. That was £30,000 in total and I wasn't having any of it.

'Seriously, Raze,' said Harry, 'what are you appealing for? Don't be a cunt, son. I'll tell you what, give the club a grand and we'll say no more about it.'

'No Harry, you can fuck right off,' I said. 'I ain't giving you lot a penny.' For some reason this had pissed me off quite a bit so I decided to dig my heels in.

To argue my case I decided to hire a barrister, but not just any old barrister. I wanted the world's most expensive barrister, who happened to live in Johannesburg. I was confident I'd win the case and if I did the club would have to pay all the costs. Doddle. After getting in touch with this bloke, who appeared to specialise in getting famous people out of tight situations

– finding loopholes, basically – he told me how much it would cost.

'Fuck me,' I said to him. 'Really?'

'And there are my expenses,' he said. 'I will require first-class return travel and an executive room at the Dorchester Hotel for one week. There will also be other expenses such as food, drink and taxis.'

'Whatever you want, son,' I said to him. Well, the club were going to be paying. What did I care?

I met this bloke a couple of times at the Dorchester and he was knocking back the Bollinger like there was no tomorrow. God only knows how much it was costing.

When it came to the day of the hearing I was quietly confident, as was my barrister. I later found out that Harry was even more confident as beforehand he'd spoken to Dave Richards from the FA, who was heading the three-man panel, and after looking at all the evidence he'd told Harry that I stood no chance. We'd have to see, wouldn't we?

Until then, all I'd seen my barrister do was eat lobster, drink Bollinger and talk with a funny accent, but when he got up to interview Harry and Peter Barnes, who was the secretary at West Ham, I realised exactly why he could demand basically whatever he wanted. He tied them both in knots! I've never seen anything so savage in my entire life. At the end of it you could tell that Harry and Peter didn't know what had hit them, and even the three blokes on the panel looked shellshocked. Whatever Harry and Peter said he just destroyed them. It was embarrassing. Not for me though. I was as chuffed to fucking bits and when the barrister had finished with them and came to sit down I gave him a big pat in the back. 'Get in, my son,' I said.

After a quick deliberation Dave Richards said that they had no choice other than to overturn the decision. When he delivered the verdict to the parties nobody seemed surprised, least of all Harry and Peter.

'Unlucky, H,' I said, looking over at my manager. I tried not to appear too smug but it wasn't easy. He and Peter were still recovering from the hammering they'd just taken from my South African rottweiler and I'm not sure the verdict had sunk in yet.

A few minutes later the barrister handed me an envelope. 'These are my expenses in full,' he said, 'including my fee.' I opened the envelope and almost shat my pants. Forty fucking grand!

'Bloody hell,' I said to him. 'I'm in the wrong business.' That was about the closest I came to making the bugger smile.

After popping the invoice back into its envelope I handed it straight back to him. 'I think you'll find the loser pays costs,' I said, pointing at Peter and Harry. 'Give it to those two.'

After walking over to his victims and handing them the envelope, Peter opened it, showed it to Harry and then handed it back to the barrister. 'This isn't a court of law, Razor, you have to pay your own expenses.' As the enormity of this was sinking in, Harry looked at me, gave me a little wink and said, 'Unlucky, Raze.'

I was ten grand down! Harry told this story at the Royal Albert Hall a few years ago and it brought the house down. The moral of this story, by the way, is don't be a bloody prick.

24

Never Judge a Book, or a Footballer

One of the biggest shocks I've ever had on a football field happened shortly after Fabrizio Ravanelli joined Boro for about £7 million in 1996. I know he'd played for Juventus and all that but for some reason I'd never heard of him, and when I saw him on the telly I thought he looked like an old-aged pensioner. *Look at the state of that*, I thought to myself. *They've bought somebody's dad by mistake!* He was also on about £44,000 a week – in 1996! You could get a lot of meals-on-wheels for that.

Anyway, Liverpool had Boro the first game of the season at the Riverside and to be honest with you I thought it would be a rout. They had a few decent players but they also had some not so decent ones and so I think we were pretty confident. What happened? Granddad ended up scoring a fucking hat-trick and we ended up drawing the game 3–3. I remember the Boro fans singing a song to the tune of 'Macarena'. It went, 'When he scores a goal he shows off his belly, HEEEEY RAVANELLI!' I was fucking dumbstruck. At the return fixture at Anfield, by which time he'd scored about a hundred bloody goals, I managed to get his gloves for my boy. Gloves, in December? Mind you, old people feel the cold more, so I've heard.

Actually, that wasn't my first big shock on a football field. It was 1992, when I was at Spurs, and Leeds had recently bought some French idiot called Eric Cantona. *Eric?* I thought. *Eric-tion more like.* He looked like a right prick. We ended up getting thumped, this time 5–0, and he scored three of them. A couple of months later Alex Ferguson snapped him up and I ended up feeling his collar. That was a fucking shock though. Bloody Cantona!

In 2001 we, as in Liverpool, were playing PSG in the UEFA Cup and they'd just bought some Brazilian kid called Ronaldinho. As well as having a ridiculous mop of curly hair he looked like he didn't have any teeth so what was he going to do, gum us to death? Seriously, he looked like a fucking cunt, an ugly one at that. We got done 2–0 and he scored both. Great, thanks for coming. He gave me twisted blood, that bloke.

One of the questions people often ask me, apart from when was the last time you saw your cock, is what was the best period of your career and I always say the last six months of my Liverpool career. In fact, it was the greatest six months of my life and for two reasons. Number one, I used to share a room with Jamie Redknapp, which was interesting (he's got some lovely clothes), and number two, I was getting twenty grand a week and Saturdays off!

I'll tell you what, while we're on the subject of shocks, let's do the greatest goal I ever scored, which believe me was a massive shock, especially to me! It was the 1993–4 season and we were playing at home against the old enemy, Man United. We were trailing 3–2 at the time and there wasn't long on the clock. Subsequently, I was absolutely fucking knackered and was coasting on fumes. We ended up getting a breakaway and the only reason I was in the Man United box was because I hadn't made it back after the last attack. I was just starting to set off actually and before I got to the halfway line we got the ball and came back. 'Oh for fuck's sake!' I said.

I started running back towards their goal and the only reason I was still going when the ball came in was because I couldn't actually stop! Heeeeelp! I pretended that Gary Pallister and me had clashed heads after the goal so I wouldn't have to carry on. It was a very convincing performance as it goes and, best of all, it worked! I watched the highlights from the match the other day and I get all kinds of plaudits from Andy Gray. After I've scored the goal he says, 'What a huge part Ruddock plays. He's the one who fed Bjørnebye and then he didn't hang around!' Really? I don't remember that. In fact, I don't remember any of it really. I was too knackered!

Actually, that's not the best goal I ever scored. The best goal I ever scored was against Cambridge University away. I was playing for Tottenham reserves and the crowd consisted of about three blokes and a dead dog. Their goalkeeper booted it while I was standing on the halfway line and without letting it bounce I chested it, kneed it and then volleyed it back over his head and into the back of the net. I shit you not! That's exactly what happened. People always assume it's Man United at home, 1993–4, but it's not, it's Cambridge University away, 1987, I think!

Another question people often ask me is who would play me in a film and I have an answer for that. Or rather a story with an answer in it. I was playing for West Ham and one night me, Wrighty, Frank, Rio, Julian Dicks and about three others went up west on the piss. We'd got ourselves a minibus for the night and after causing a bit of chaos in the usual haunts we piled back in and said, 'Home James!' When we were about a mile away from the training ground, which is where we were going to catch our respective taxis, we passed a lovely little kebab van.

'STOOOOOOOOOOP!' I ordered. 'I take it everyone's in. Chilli sauce?'

After jumping out and putting in our order these two birds came up to me. 'It's you, innit?' one of them said.

'Yes ladies,' I replied. 'It is indeed – *moi*.' By this time, the lads had piled out of the minibus. 'I take it you're fans then?'

'Ooh, not 'arf,' said the other one. 'We've been watching *London's Burning* for donkey's years, haven't we Shirl? I must say, though, you look older than you do on the telly.'

'Eh? I think you might be mistaken, girls. I'm a professional footballer. Razor Ruddock? West Ham, Liverpool, England?'

'Oh, Christ,' said Shirl. 'We can't stand football. You're all a bunch of 'ooligans,' and with that they just pissed off.

The lads ruined me big time for this and after collecting my kebab I exited stage left. The actor they were referring to was called Glen Murphy and, after looking him up on the inter-whatsit, it appears he was born in West Ham, so I suppose he'd be good at playing me. Then again, he's about ten years older than me.

How about Mr Blonde from *Reservoir Dogs*? Michael Madsen. He looks a bit like me. Then again, could he do the London accent? I doubt it. Not without sounding like Dick Van Dyke.

Nope, at the end of the day the person best equipped to play the fucking legend that is Neil 'Razor' Ruddock is Neil 'Razor' Ruddock and I'm not going to need any acting lessons. I've been acting like a prick for over half a century and I've got it down to a fine art.

25

Retirement

I don't know what it's like now but when I was a player we used to get a pension at thirty-five years of age and, if I'm being brutally honest, which I am some of the time, I couldn't wait for my thirty-fifth birthday. My knees were knackered, I was struggling with my weight and, do you know what, I just wasn't enjoying it any more.

One of the reasons I consider myself to have been extremely lucky in life isn't because I used to earn a shedload of money, it's because I was able to do what I loved for a living. If I'd been paid £200 a week to do it, I'd have been fine with that. These days it's different. I'm not saying for one moment that all footballers are only in it for the money but there's no escaping the fact that money is more of a deciding factor these days, and a love of the game, whether it's there or not, will usually take a back seat.

When my thirty-fifth birthday finally came and I retired, the first thing I did was breathe a massive sigh of relief. Then, after pouring myself one or ten massive drinks, I started playing a lot of golf. The novelty of all this lasted about a month and then slowly but surely I started to miss certain parts of my old life. I certainly didn't miss the training and I didn't really miss playing that much either. What I did miss was the company of the other lads and the longer I was away from the dressing room the harder I tried to compensate, and the harder I tried to compensate, the more fucked up I became. It's no wonder three out of five footballers get divorced within two or three years of retiring.

It's also no surprise that the only part of the job I really missed was the camaraderie and friendship. A lot of people are under the misapprehension that the life of a footballer is just a massive bed of roses but, although we're obviously very well paid and well looked after, there are certain aspects that, especially if you've got a family, take some of the shine off. For instance, going away for a summer holiday with the wife and kids was always nigh on impossible when I was playing as just when the kids were breaking up for the holidays we'd be reporting back for pre-season training. Then there's Christmas and New Year. Unless you're injured, you'll spend a large part of that period either stuck in a hotel room or on a plane. So, if you play until you're thirty-five and have a family, the chances are those times – which are supposed to be magical times – will have passed you by. In that respect, it's the kids I feel the sorriest for, but at the end of the day every job has its ups and downs. I have friends who love what they do, earn a decent living and have always been able to spend Christmas and New Year with their families and take a nice long summer holiday. That, to me, is real wealth.

Instead of continuing to play golf and trying to find something else, such as coaching or commentating, to occupy my time, I reverted to being a teenager again. Except instead of training every day, playing every weekend and watching what I ate and drank, I was left to my own devices. That, when you've got a few quid in your pocket and are missing your old mates, is a recipe for disaster. Within a few months I was going on benders lasting two or three days.

As well as my pension, offers like *I'm a Celebrity . . . Get Me Out of Here!* would come along every so often and top up my bank balance. Providing I could behave myself for the duration of them, which I could, the self-destruction would be put on hold for a few weeks and then once they were over I'd just dive back in and carry on as normal.

After about a year or so I ended up in rehab for a couple of weeks. That was for addiction, which wasn't really my problem. I didn't touch a drop in the jungle and, if I was at home, I could take it or leave it. The trouble was I never was at home and had started to put my drinking mates before my family. If I was addicted to anything it was going out and having a good time. It got that bad that if I had to choose between letting my mates down or my family down, the family would always lose. That's when I knew that I'd really hit rock bottom and it ended up costing me my first marriage.

One of the greatest lessons I've ever learned in life is how to enjoy the company of my wife and kids. When I was playing football that was alien to me and, because we never had the Christmases and the summer holidays, it never really occurred to me. It was a case of what you never have you never miss. The fact that I've been given a second chance by having two more kids with Leah is probably a lot more than I deserve. I'm a lucky man.

Rehab was interesting, despite me being there for the wrong reasons. We did something called the Twelve Steps and the therapist we had was a northern lad from Sheffield. One of the steps was talking about the most embarrassing thing you've ever done and his approach was to try and shock us into being truthful by telling us about the most embarrassing thing he'd ever done.

'Have you ever had a wank over your brother's wife?' he said. 'I have.'

'Hang on,' I replied. 'Do you mean over her as in "all over her", or over her, as in, when you're delving into the old wank bank?'

That shut him up, at least for a few seconds.

'Erm, the latter,' he said finally.

'Oh, right then. Sorry, I thought you meant have I ever had a wank over my brother's wife in person.'

'No, of course that's not what I meant!' he said, alarmed. 'That would be disgusting.'

'If you say so.'

It seemed like I'd beaten him at his own game but to be fair to the lad he decided to have another go.

'All right then,' he said, 'have you ever shagged a chicken?'

'Why?' I said. 'Have you?'

'Yes I fucking have,' he said. 'Out of my mum's freezer!'

'Fuck me,' I said. 'You and me had better swap places! Look mate, if you want me to trust you and open up, telling me that you've shagged a frozen chicken that you've taken from your mum's freezer – I take it you didn't put it back? – and have had a J. Arthur Rank over your brother's wife isn't the way to go about it. In fact, I don't think I really belong here.'

I did thirty meetings in thirty days and they were all pretty similar. One women said, in all seriousness, 'I'd drop my knickers for half a lager and blackcurrant!' and instead of sitting there being understanding and looking solemn like everyone else I broke down in hysterics.

'What would you do for a pint, a chaser and a packet of pork scratchings?' I asked.

'That isn't very helpful, Neil,' said the therapist.

I just couldn't take the meetings seriously, which fits with my theory that I'd regressed to being a teenager again. What a tit.

Now that I'm retired, one thing I would like to get more involved in is mental health. When I started out in football it was a taboo subject and especially for men. In fact, I'm not even sure the term mental health was used when I was a lad. You were either mad or you were sane. In football it was obviously no different and, as with the world at large, if you had a problem in that department you kept it to yourself. I honestly dread to think how many footballers suffered in silence over the years. Many thousands, probably. It's a horrible thought.

Fortunately, things are very different these days and, as far as I'm concerned, the longer mental health remains a hot topic in football the better. Ironically, admitting you had a problem upstairs was seen as a sign of weakness when I was young when in actual fact it's the opposite. It's all to do with creating an environment in which people are comfortable talking about their troubles and, although I've never suffered to the extent of other players, I have seen at first-hand what it can do.

How times have changed though. At the risk of sounding like an old fart, when I first went to Liverpool we didn't even have a physio. I shit you not! All we had was Ronnie Moran, a few ice baths and an ultrasound machine. I was actually the dearest defender in the world when I signed at £2.5 million (until Des Walker went to Sheffield Wednesday for £3.9 million the day after, the wanker) and when I turned up at Anfield for the first time I actually had a bad knee. Ronnie Moran was the coach and he said, 'Come with me, Razor. Let's do an ultrasound on it.'

Ultrasound, I thought. *That sounds good!*

Unfortunately, Ronnie had run out of the gel you're supposed to put on first and so instead he got some Fairy Liquid from the kitchen.

'Here, this'll do,' he said, squirting some on my knee.

'Are you sure?' I said. I was the most expensive defender in the world and I was having a Fairy Liquid ultrasound on my knee!

These days my knee would be looked at by about six different people and had I needed treatment I'd have been taken to hospital on a sedan chair, had rose petals thrown in front of me and been fed grapes by really fit virgins!

I'll tell you something else that was different at Liverpool, but this was for the better. When I was at Spurs before that we were paid win bonuses per game. Mine was about five grand per win so it was a good whack. At Liverpool there was none of that. You got £25 a point and that was it. They used to say, 'Why the hell should we pay you to win? That's what you're paid to try and do in the first place!' It was a fair point.

The chief exec, Peter Robinson, was a right shrewd bastard. About two years before Sky came in and started throwing all the dosh around he got us all on five-year contracts with decent money. We all thought we were quids in but when the wages became enormous we were all stuck on five-year contracts! I remember thinking, you clever fucker. As I said, he was a right shrewd bastard. At the end of the day though, that's exactly what he was paid to do.

26

Welcome to the Jungle

B ecause of my gob, my nickname, my good looks and my reputation, I was always going to be fodder for these kind of reality shows and when I retired from being a footballer the offers came in thick and fast. What's more, I absolutely loved them and still do. The money's always good and you get to meet some interesting people. And one or two tossers.

The first one to come along was *I'm a Celebrity . . . Get Me out of Here!* in 2004. This wasn't too long after I'd retired and the offer was basically to see if I would like to spend a few weeks in Australia with some other celebrities while camping out in the jungle. It was a no-brainer as far as I was concerned. There'd be no training, which was good, and I figured it would be a walk in the park. Or in the jungle. The other celebs taking part were Peter Andre, Kerry Katona, Jennie Bond, Lord Brocket, Katie Price, Alex Best, John Lydon, Mike Read and Diane Modahl. At first glance, it didn't seem like a bad bunch and, despite what I'd seen and heard, I was really looking forward to it.

The main piece of advice I remember them giving us before we were all released into the jungle was, 'Do not go near black spiders and brown snakes because they can kill you.' That made everyone squeak a bit, I can tell you. If you did get bitten by one of these things you had about half an hour to live and they obviously had a doctor stationed close by with an antidote. My main problem with this was that I don't like spiders. In fact, I'm a bigger arachnophobe than I am an arsehole, and some of the spiders were as big as my hand. The first time I had a run in with one of them was in the toilet. Or the dunny, as they call it. This was quite lucky really as I always shit myself when I see a spider, except there wasn't just one of them, there was about twenty! The toilet had a piece of tarpaulin for a roof and if it was night time you had to use a candle. I woke up wanting a number two so lit a candle and made my way over there. Some of the noises you hear in the jungle would make your hair curl, especially at night. In fact, the snoring, which came from everywhere, used to drown them out a bit so it was actually quite comforting.

When I reached my destination I put my hand holding the candle into the doorway of the dunny so it lit the place up and the first thing I saw were about twenty spiders crawling on the tarpaulin. Fortunately, they were brown as opposed to black but I still had to try and get rid of the fuckers before I could sit down. Could you imagine sitting down for a crap with twenty huge spiders hanging over you? Just the thought of it makes my skin crawl. I waved the candle round a bit and wobbled the tarpaulin and eventually they buggered off. That was the quickest crap I've ever had, though, by a mile.

If ever you did see a black spider or a brown snake you had to shout and after turning off the cameras an aboriginal gentleman would run into the camp and sort them out. Then, once it was safe again, he'd bugger off and they'd turn on the cameras again.

On I think the third night I was on fire watch (if the fire goes out you're fucked so you take it in turns to make sure it doesn't) when all of a sudden I looked around and there, about two yards away from me, was a king brown snake, which is one of the ones they'd warned us about. *Shit a brick*, I thought. *I'm a goner!* The only piece of advice they'd given us for this situation was to act like a tree and I was shaking that much that it didn't really seem plausible. A tree with a bear inside it taking a shit, perhaps? One thing you're not supposed to do if a snake's that close is start shouting so I actually just sat there and did nothing. Fortunately, it decided to move on, and after passing under the log I was sitting on it went off in the direction of Kerry Katona. Because it was now close to Kerry, I still couldn't shout and thank fuck she remained asleep because if she hadn't she'd have been toast. The snake literally went within an inch of her face and it even waggled its tongue in front of her. Would you give a Frenchie to a king brown snake? I wouldn't. Not unless it was holding the kitty.

After what was probably the longest few seconds of my life the snake pissed off down a giant rat hole and as soon as it had gone I raised the alarm. 'SNAAAAAAAAAAAAAAAAAAKE! THERE'S A FUCKING SNAAAAAAAAAAAAAAAAKE!'

The aboriginal gentleman was on the scene in seconds and, after I pointed to the rat hole, he went over and actually put his hand down it.

'What the bloody hell are you doing?' I hissed.

'I'm trying to grab the snake, you idiot,' said the snake man. 'Snakes can't turn around in tight spaces. It's perfectly safe.' Perfectly safe my arse. This man was a fucking lunatic! 'Are you sure it was a king brown?' asked the snake man.

'Absolutely,' I said.

'OK. You know that if it bites me I've got half an hour to live,' he said reassuringly. 'But it's OK. The doctor with the antidote is just a few minutes away.'

Suddenly, John Lydon sat up and said, 'So what if the doctor gets bitten by a king brown on the way here? Who's he going to give the antidote to? It won't be you, mate.'

He pulled his hand out a bit sharpish after that.

One day we were playing golf with a tree branch and a cone when out of the corner of my eye I saw a yellow spider about the size of my hand. This hadn't been on the danger list but even so I wasn't taking chances.

'SPIDER!' I shouted. 'SPIDER AS BIG AS MY FUCKING HAND. GET HIM OVER HERE. COME ON, I CAN'T PLAY GOLF WITH THAT THING STARING AT ME.'

This thing had red and blue dots on it and when the aboriginal gentleman arrived he took one look at it and said, 'I've never seen one of them before. Nope. Sorry.' Then, he just picked up a tree branch, put it next to the spider, the spider jumped on and away they went. Happy as Larry. What a nutter!

The rats there are the size of bloody cats. I shit you not. You know how you kick a cat off your bed when it jumps on? Well, these things would do the same and you'd literally just kick them off. You're so tired, though, that even if you're scared of rats you don't have the energy to make a fuss and you can't shit yourself because you haven't eaten. What's the point of being scared if you can't shit yourself?

My original idea after being offered the show had been to do a few hours and then say to the producers, 'Look, lads, this isn't for me. I think I'll just hop on a plane back to England

and keep all your lovely dosh.' That little scheme lasted about two minutes as we were informed before we left that if you walked out of the show you wouldn't get paid. If you were voted off first you got all your money, but if you walked out, it was *nada*. I was one of the favourites to win at the start, naturally, but as the days went on I lost more and more weight – eighteen pounds in eleven days to be exact, and that was just sitting on my arse – and because of that I found it more and more difficult to get involved in anything. After about day nine I had to be put on a drip and they said that if I hadn't improved by the following day I'd have to go. Unfortunately, I hadn't improved and so they blocked all my telephone lines and that was it.

One of the reasons I fancied myself to do well on the show was because I'll eat anything, and I figured that if I was prepared to eat anything then I wouldn't get voted off. I knew that all the women would be as fussy as hell, you see, so I thought I'd be a shoo-in. One of the challenges I remember was having a big glass bowl put over my head and then it being filled with lots of creepy crawlies. That didn't bother me really and it was just mind over matter. I'm not saying it was nice. It wasn't! The smell was unbelievable. Later on, it got to a point where I physically couldn't do the challenges and that's when the drip came in.

What an experience though. As hard as it became I loved every single second of that show and I'd do it again in a flash. I'm not sure I could do the heights thing. We never had to do that bit. Give me a kangaroo's testicle or a live grub, though, and I'll munch away like a good'un.

Sometime after that I got an offer to appear on *Celebrity Big Brother*, although that was at the eleventh hour. Jim Davidson was supposed to have been going on but he had to pull out at the last minute and they decided to call me. I think I'm one of the only men to have appeared on both *I'm a Celebrity* and *Celebrity Big Brother*. Loads of women have done it but I have the feeling I might actually be the only bloke. Some clever fucker will probably write in and tell me if I'm not.

So, what can I tell you about *Celebrity Big Brother*? Well, for a start, it's a piece of piss, that much I do know. In fact, it's the opposite of *I'm a Celebrity* because as opposed to starving you and giving you challenges they just feed you and give you alcohol and fags. Basically, you get a load of money for sitting around on your arse all day talking bollocks. Some of the other contestants would start whingeing about being bored and I'd say, 'You're getting paid a fortune, you cunt, and you're moaning about being bored? Would you rather be standing in a factory packing boxes? No, of course you wouldn't. So shut your fucking mouth, you dickhead.'

On the celebrity version they ply you with booze, which obviously loosens people's tongues and, as anyone who's ever watched the show will tell you, it works a treat. Among the celebs appearing on my series were Rylan Clark-Neal, who was the eventual winner and still thinks I'm his dad, Claire Richards from Steps, Frankie Dettori, Gillian Taylforth from *EastEnders* and Tricia Penrose who was in *Heartbeat*. The reason Rylan thinks I'm his dad is because I was playing for Tottenham when he was born, and his dad obviously looks and sounds just like me. He was a very worthy winner in my opinion and his career has obviously gone from strength to strength. He ended up being the ring bearer at my wedding to Leah, which was nice. He should have been a bridesmaid though.

The only people I didn't really warm to in the house were the aptly named Spencer Pratt and his other half Heidi Montag, who hadn't really done much and were about as interesting as a used teabag. On the other end of the scale, in both likeability and talent, was Claire from Steps. I got on like a house on fire with her and when we first met she came out with a blinder.

'Hello,' I said, 'my name's Razor.'

'Hello,' she said, 'my name's Claire. I've sold ten million records worldwide.'

I thought, *Come here you!* I thought that was brilliant. I also got on very well with Frankie Dettori, who again had reached the very top of his profession.

The thing with Spencer, who I really did not like, came to a head one night when, in my opinion, he was bullying Claire. I called him out about this but instead of shutting his gob he started acting all hard so I told him I was going to kill him, or words to that effect. It was no idle threat. He was giving me the right hump and I was desperate to give him a slap. In the end, his other half realised what was going to happen and called in security, and it all died down after that. As I just said, alcohol gets thrown around like water in there and people who wouldn't normally socialise with each other outside the house quite often clash.

Anyway, the day after the series had finished we all had a get together and early on the evening Spencer came running up to me with Dettori in tow.

'Razor!' he said. 'I hear from Frankie that your family are one of the most powerful in London. Is that true? They can open doors, apparently.'

I obviously had no idea what the little dickhead was talking about but as he spoke Dettori was over his shoulder mouthing at me to go along with it, and so I did. 'Oh, my family,' I said, starting to get into character. 'Well, yes. They do have a certain reputation. Not to mention a certain amount of influence.'

'But what about your brothers, Razor?' said Frankie. 'They're going to kill Spencer when he gets out. You have to call them off!' Frankie was being deadly serious and Spencer obviously believed him.

'Shit,' I said. 'I never thought of that. Fuck me, Spencer, Frankie's right. Because you were acting like such a dickhead in there, the chances are they'll be waiting for you. Frankie, for fuck's sake go and call them!'

By this time Spencer's sweating like a flasher in a bush and just as I'm filling him in about the Ruddock crime dynasty Frankie comes running back in. 'I've managed to call them off,' he said. 'Until tomorrow!'

The following morning Spencer called me up. 'Razor, would you and your family like to come to the Dorchester Hotel for lunch? My treat.'

'Well Spence,' I said, becoming all hard and mysterious again, 'the family are a little bit busy today. Know what I mean?'

'Of course,' he said. 'No problem, Razor.'

I could tell he was terrified. To this day Spencer Pratt thinks my family run London, and all thanks to Frankie Dettori.

Another cultural gem I had the good fortune to be involved in was *Celebrity Wife Swap*, in which me and my wife Leah 'swapped' with the late Pete Burns, from the band Dead or Alive, and his husband, Michael. When the offer came through for that one we didn't even have to think about it, although I have to admit that I'd been expecting it to be a straight swap, if you see what I mean, as in me being swapped for somebody else's husband and Leah being swapped for somebody else's wife.

They obviously don't tell you who you're being swapped with and on the first day of filming they took Leah off to the house belonging to the other couple and they sent me down to the pub. The plan was that while I was down there having a few my new wife could move into our place and make herself comfortable, but after four hours I was still sitting there.

'Look, mate,' I said to the producer, 'I'm going to be shit-faced if she don't hurry up.'

'You could always try drinking something soft,' he replied.

Talk about an improper suggestion!

Fortunately, about ten minutes later we got the call that my new wife had arrived at Chez Ruddock and was ready to receive me. I was actually quite nervous at this point as all of a sudden it had become a bit real and I did start to worry if me and the new missus would get on. At the end of the day they want drama on these shows and I had visions of walking into my living room and being confronted by some teetotal feminist who hates football and swearing.

When I got to the house I walked through the front door, and through a gap in the door leading to the living room I could see somebody wearing high heels. *Aye aye*, I thought. *I've got a dolly bird here!* I felt so much better.

As I turned the corner into the living room I started to look up and it was only when I saw his face that I realised I'd got it wrong. For anyone who doesn't know, Pete Burns was a Scouser who could obviously look after himself and despite looking extremely feminine he had quite a deep voice. This was made apparent to me when he opened his mouth for the first time and said, 'All right, dickhead. I'm going to fuck you.'

What an opener!

As I was pissing myself laughing the director shouted, 'Cut! Can you do that again please, but this time without the swearing?'

Here we go, I thought. *Bearing in mind what I'm like we could be in for a long week!*

When I walked back into the living room for take two Pete said in a very posh voice, 'Oh hello, I'm Peter. So pleased to meet you. What's your name?'

'Cut!'

It was already clear that Pete Burns did not like being told what to do and, because I'm a little bit like that myself, the TV people must already have been thinking, *What the hell have we done?* It also became clear quite early on that they'd been expecting fireworks but the fact is we got on like a house on fire. My daughter Pebbles was in the house and Pete was fabulous with her, and with me, although I never let him fuck me.

It got to a point where Peter and I had to take the TV people to one side and say, 'Look, what do you want us to do?'

'Could you have an argument please?'

'Of course we can. Pete, you're a bone idle twat.'

'You fuckin what? I'll fucking do you!'

It was a case of never judge a book by its cover, or in this case two books. They obviously thought I was just a thick Neanderthal footballer who would rather stick pins in his eyes than share a house with a man who dressed as a woman, and that Pete and I would hate each other. Unlucky, fuckers!

Pete Burns was one of the most kind, interesting and funny people I've ever met in my life. From the moment he told me he was going to fuck me I knew we'd get on. I said to him a bit later, 'If it makes good television, Pete, I'll let yer.'

'Oh, it'll make good television, Razor,' he said. 'You mark my words!'

He used to knock on my door at night and go, 'Razooooor, are you there? I'm gonna fuck yooooooooou!'

In all seriousness, I'd rather have let him fuck me than fight me. Peter wasn't small (especially in heels) and he was as strong as a fucking ox. Also, because of all the shit he'd had to take over the years for being different, he'd had to learn to look after himself. The stories he told me about some of the scrapes he got into would make your teeth itch. He was like Jimmy Case in drag!

The highlight of my week with the late and much missed Pete Burns was when I asked if I could go down the pub to watch England play. I'm pretty sure it was a Euro 2008 qualifier and when I asked him he said, 'You can go,' he said. 'But only if you have colonic irrigation.'

I'd been expecting either a yes or a no, with the possibility of him asking me to do the washing up first. One thing I hadn't been expecting after asking to watch the football was him suggest that somebody shove a pipe up my arse first.

'Go on, Raze,' he said. 'I reckon you'll enjoy it. And anyway, you're not watching the football here. I've got the remote. It's your choice.'

One of the rules of *Celebrity Wife Swap* was that I had to do as I was told and so Pete had me over a barrel, so to speak. It was a qualifier though and the thought of missing the match was unthinkable. I was going to have to say yes. 'Go on then,' I said. 'What do I have to do?' Talk about taking one for the fucking team!

I had to lie on my side and after sticking a pipe up my arse someone – not Pete, he just stood and watched – started filling me up with coffee, of all things.

'Hang on,' said the woman doing the deed suddenly. 'The pipe's come out. Let me just push it in again.' Just as she did that Pete leant over and said, 'Nice that, innit Raze?'

Unfortunately, I just couldn't stop laughing which is why the pipe had come out and a few seconds later it happened again.

'Let's have another go shall we, Razor?' said the irrigator. When the pipe went in again Pete leant over for the second time and said, 'Nice that, innit Raze?'

In the end they had to put Sellotape around the pipe just to keep it up my arse. I'll tell you what though, I felt miles better afterwards. I obviously couldn't sleep for a week as I was full up with caffeine, but I skipped down the pub like a new man. These days I refuse to watch a game of football without being irrigated first.

Go on, have a go. You'll love it.

27

The Greatest Night of
My Sporting Life!

If I tell you that the greatest night of my sporting life took place in Wolverhampton you'll probably think I scored a hat-trick against Wolves or something. Wrong! It was at the Grand Slam of Darts, which always takes place in Wolverhampton. The night before the first day they held a pro-celebrity mixed doubles tournament, which I was invited to take part in. Before it started they drew the names of the players and the celebrities out of a hat and I was paired with Phil 'The Power' Taylor. Not a bad draw!

We played first to three legs and after chucking some abso-lutely blistering darts we found ourselves in the semi-final. To be fair to Phil, he also chucked a few good'uns and I was pleased he was there. In the semi-final we played Wayne 'Hawaii 501' Mardle and Michael Le Vell who plays Kevin Webster in *Coronation Street*. To be brutally honest, until that point Phil had carried me in every single leg. I'd played OK in the practice room but on the stage I lost it. There were three thousand people in that hall and each and every one of them was three sheets to the wind. What's more, they all seemed to support football teams other than the ones I'd played for, and whenever I stepped up to the oche the noise went into overdrive. On a football field that wouldn't have bothered me one bit but here I was out of my comfort zone. I think the crowd could smell blood.

Somehow, despite me averaging something like fifteen, we managed to get it to 2–2 and in the deciding leg Phil threw some amazing arrows to leave me on double top. Wayne Mardle was following me and wanted double sixteen, his favourite.

'Razor Ruddock,' said the ref, 'you require forty.'

When I stepped up to the oche I was shaking like a shitting dog and the crowd were giving me all sorts.

'Quiet please,' said the referee.

Unbelievably the crowd did as they were told. As I stood there at the oche and reached for my first dart I could actually hear my heart beating. It was horrible! In the end I decided that I felt more comfortable with the noise so I turned around, walked to the front of the stage and went 'COME ON, YER CUNTS!'

As you'd expect, the place just erupted and without even stopping I walked straight back to the oche, threw my dart and it went straight into the middle of double top.

'THAT'S GAME, SET AND THE MATCH TO PHIL TAYLOR AND RAZOR RUDDOCK!'

I threw my other two darts into the wall and when I turned around Phil was on his knees giving it the old 'We Are Not Worthy.' That was, as the title of this chapter suggests, the greatest sporting moment of my entire fucking life. We had to get a step ladder to take my darts out of the wall, which was a giggle. I'd thrown them about five foot above the board!

Next up was the final and, unfortunately, by the time it took place, I'd had a few too many sherbets and I played like a lemon.

Our opponents were James 'The Machine' Wade and Steve Backley, the former world-record-holding javelin thrower. I thought that was a bit unfair as Steve was obviously used to throwing dart-shaped things but my complaints, which were probably incomprehensible, fell on deaf ears.

I think I averaged about seven in that match and we got done three zip. Phil was furious, partly because he doesn't like losing and obviously isn't used to it, but also because we were getting five grand a win. I'll tell you what, though, what a fucking player that man is. In the practice room before the tournament we played a match where he started on 501 and I started on 301. To make it more interesting, he stood twice as far away from the board as I did, so over fifteen foot! He still ended up thrashing me and I didn't even get a dart at a double. Next up they covered the board with paper and Phil and Wayne took it in turns to ask the celebrities which number they wanted them to hit. 'Hit seven,' I'd ask. Bang, in. It was just incredible.

Yep. You can keep your Wembleys and you can keep your Anfields an' all. Wolverhampton Civic Hall, 2008. The greatest night of my sporting life.

28

The Wake-up Call

One of the most recent TV shows I've appeared on is *Harry's Heroes: Euro Having a Laugh.* That was a bit of a turning point for me as it's when the full extent of my physical problems started to become apparent – to me, at least. To everyone else it was common knowledge apparently but I'd just ignored it. For instance, I was told after the first series that I was pre-diabetic and in my mind if I was pre-diabetic that meant I wasn't a diabetic. That was the attitude I'd always taken to things like health and whenever people tried to pull me up on it I'd tell them to piss off. Or words to that effect.

A couple of weeks before we were due to start filming the second series of *Harry's Heroes,* I had a bit of a turn. I was running upstairs for some reason – probably for a dump – and suddenly felt a bit giddy. Bloody hell, I thought. Something's not right here. At first I thought it might have been because I'd headed so many balls and that panicked me a bit. I just ignored it, though, and went off to film the series.

I'll come on to what happened with Paul Merson and the series itself in a second but after being taken off the series I was sent to see a German bloke called Dr Grotta on Harley Street. Anyone who thinks that Germans don't have a sense of humour should meet this bloke. He's hilarious! Anyway, after running some initial tests he found out that my resting heartrate was 130 beats per minute, which is roughly what it should be during a high-intensity workout.

'Das is not good, Herr Ruddock,' said Dr Grotta. What was even more alarming was the fact that my heart was stopping for up to seven seconds every night. 'Das also is not good, Herr Ruddock,' said the doctor. 'You are effectively dying every night. Like a shit comedian.'

That was a bit of a shock, I can tell you.

Speaking of which . . . in order to get my heart back on an even keel again they first had to stop it and start it again, and to do that they used a defibrillator.

'How many times have you done this?' I said to the doctor.

'This is my first time,' he said. 'But it's OK. I've Googled it.'

I was pissing myself laughing, which, given what was happening to my ticker, probably wasn't ideal.

After stopping my heart and starting it again, they fitted a pacemaker. These days my resting heartrate's about 70, which is as it should be. Had *Harry's Heroes* not happened I'd have been brown bread according to Dr Grotta, so I'm obviously glad it did.

I could be wrong but I'd say the vast majority of people reading this will probably have seen the incident involving me and Merse, and if you haven't seen it the chances are you'll have read or heard about it. Despite me having dizzy spells, I was still in denial about what might be happening to me physically and, when you put someone like me on a coach with a load of former footballers who like a drink or ten and then send me off into Europe with a few quid in my pocket, only one thing's going to happen. Basically, you get right on it, which is exactly what we did.

Merse's own problems with alcohol and gambling are well documented and at the time of filming he hadn't had a drink or a bet for quite a few months. When he saw me knocking them back he feared for my health, just as he must have feared for his own health when he was in the depths. I think the difference was that Merse is a recovering alcoholic whereas I'm just somebody who likes to have a drink, so when he became all serious about what I was doing I didn't appreciate it, which is why we had the argument. Had I been aware of my condition or had stopped to think about it from Merse's point of view then it might have been different, but as far as I was concerned I was just having a good time with my mates and I thought he was being a bit holier than thou. More than anything, it was nine o'clock in the fucking morning when it happened, and if you want to take me to task about something – anything, in fact – it's best to wait until after midday and/or until my hangover's cleared. Just a word to the wise there. The only person who can get away with having a go earlier is my missus and in that situation I just have to grin and bear it. 'Yes, dear. Anything you say, dear. Of course, dear.'

The only reason I didn't fly off the handle with Merse and have a proper go is because I love the man to bits. What's more, I remember what he was like when he was in the grips of his alcoholism and gambling addiction, and the end of the day it was all done with the best of intentions – at nine o'clock in the fucking morning! What Merse should have done was wait until about midday and say, 'Raze, do you fancy a spot of lunch? I know this lovely little fish restaurant.' Then, over a nice plate of sea bass and a few bottles of white wine (for me, not him), he could have told me what was worrying him. I wouldn't have minded! Think on, Merse. After midday, nice little fish restaurant, sea bass, wine. OK son? Lovely.

I hadn't seen some of the lads who were on that show for over fifteen years. The thing is, when the stories start flowing it's difficult to keep up and when somebody says, 'You remember don't you, Razor? You were there,' it's best to just go, 'Yeah, of course!'

It was lovely seeing them all again, but especially Mark Wright, or Blanka, as we call him. Do you remember the video game, *Street Fighter*? Well, there used to be a green monster with ginger hair on it called Blanka and somebody must have thought it resembled Mark. That boy has an absolute heart of gold and what an amazing player. He also had a chat with me about what I'd been consuming but he decided to do it off camera. I think they wanted him to do it on camera but he said no. Blanka's like me, as in he's an old-fashioned centre half who liked kicking people and having a drink, so as much as I appreciated Merse's intervention, when Blanka had a word with me later that day it really hit home.

A couple of days after that things took a turn for the worse and I was sent to Dr Grotta, so Merse and Blanca had obviously been right to say something. I'd been a ticking time-bomb for God knows how long and, as I said, had I not gone on the show who knows what might have happened. It wouldn't have ended well, that's for sure.

So, the question you're all asking is, have I become a paragon of virtue since having my pacemaker fitted? The short answer is no, I have not. I don't go down pubs much any more and instead of getting hammered I'll have a few glasses of wine with the wife instead. With work, it's a bit different, as I do a lot of after-dinner speaking and if you're a guest at one of those every-one wants to buy you a drink. That's when it gets difficult as if somebody offers to buy me a drink – especially if they've paid to come and see me talk – I find it hard to say no. I'm also not going to say, 'Yes please, I'll have a Perrier with ya!' The point is, I always have time for people who want to have a chat. Ally McCoist taught me that. He said it doesn't matter how long it lasts, but if you have a chat with somebody for a few minutes and make eye contact it means the world to them. I've never forgotten that.

The only person who's ever mugged me off in that situation is Malcolm 'Supermac' Macdonald, who started out with Fulham before becoming a Newcastle legend, so I have actually been on the receiving end. I was playing for Southampton at the time and after spotting him in the bar I ran up to him and introduced myself. 'Hello, Mr Macdonald. My name's Neil Ruddock and I play for Southampton. My dad's a big Fulham supporter and he loves you to bits.' As I was talking he just walked off! I'm sure he didn't mean to do it but I was gutted. What is it they say, 'Manners maketh man'? Not that man!

29

Things that Might Surprise You

Because everybody thinks I'm such a fucking hard bastard, I've decided to try and put across my softer side by telling you about some of the things that shit me up and some of the things I do that might surprise you.

Let's start with what scares me. I've already told you about spiders, Graeme Souness, Sean Connery and the occasional supersize Geordie skinhead, so what else gives Razor the willies? Well, one of the big ones is heights. I fucking hate heights, almost as much as I hate skimmed milk. I mean, what the fucking hell's that all about, and what's the point? It's basically just flour and water! Heights make me feel sick and dizzy. My worst nightmare would probably be being stuck on top of a spider-infested mountain with Ian Wright and no fags. Honestly, I'd sooner go bungee jumping naked, and just the thought of that gives me the runs.

The thing that genuinely scares me the most is coming home late to the wife. Is this because I've suddenly developed a conscience, I hear you ask? Is it fuck. She's just a very scary woman who doesn't like being dicked about. I still do it, though, as in I still come in late. I don't let it bother me until I'm in the cab on the way home. Then, it starts eating away at me like I would a kebab and by the time I get to the front door

I'm a gibbering wreck. I've given up trying to make excuses. I just plead for my life instead.

Anyway, that's about it when it comes to things I'm scared of. Remember, I'm fucking hard! The question is, has the occasional glimpse of my softer side altered your opinion of me? Or do you still think I'm just a fat useless twat? Well, this might change your mind. I was on *Celebrity MasterChef* in 2019, and what's more, I got to the fucking final! That was only the second final of my entire career, by the way, including football. Being able to cook is one of the things that surprises people the most about me, not to mention the fact that I'm quite good at it. And I am, by the way.

One of the things I like most about cooking is the fact that, unlike football, it's something you can improve at no matter what you do or who you are. To somebody who always wanted to be the best footballer in the world and became frustrated when they could no longer carry on improving, that was a huge attraction. The fact that I also enjoy cooking for people – and eating, it has to be said – was a bonus. I get just as much satisfaction from making my family a meal as I did from either scoring or preventing a goal, and I can even do it when I'm hungover! Seriously, in my book cooking is the gift that keeps on giving.

One of the other reasons I like cooking is because to me there's no pressure involved, which is one of the reasons I did so well in the show. During the first round John Torode came over and asked me if I was feeling any pressure. I said, 'Mate, I promise you, this ain't pressure. This is fun. Sitting in a pub at half four in the morning when you've told your missus you're going to be home at half eleven . . . that's pressure!'

I wasn't trying to be arrogant or facetious, and I can understand fully why other contestants might have felt anxious being on the show, but at the end of the day I see cooking as a leisure activity, pure and simple, and the fact that I was on the show to improve my cooking skills made it an absolute no-brainer. What also helped me was the fact that I'd kept my expectations well in check. Don't get me wrong, I'd have loved to win the show, but my own menu was very limited so there was only so much I could do. I was, as the saying goes, just there to enjoy myself. What would spoil it for me would be doing it for a living. Being a chef is one of the hardest jobs in the world and, as far as that goes, let's just say that I'm an eater, not a worker!

On one of the episodes of *MasterChef* I had to go and work in Mere, Monica Galetti's restaurant on Charlotte Street in London, which gave me a tiny taste – pardon the pun – of what it must be like. I had to make a sauce for one of the starters and it took me four hours. I was absolutely knackered by the end of it and as much as I enjoyed the experience I was glad to get out. Keep me front-of-house, mate, and preferably at a table holding a menu!

My two biggest flaws on the show, apart from picking, which I'm very good at, were presentation and not clearing up after myself. That's what gets me into the most amount of trouble at home but once I'm in the cooking zone, that's it. I'll do the clearing up afterwards! When it came to my presentation, John Torode said to me, 'Razor, you have to remember that people eat with their eyes.'

'Not where I come from,' I said. 'Where I come from most people eat with their hands. It's not pretty but it works.'

I was beaten by Greg Rutherford in the end. A ginger fucking long jumper! Actually, that makes it a hat-trick of seconds for reality TV. Always the fucking bridesmaid!

I once did an episode of *Celebrity Come Dine with Me* which featured Carlton Palmer, Frank Worthington, me and John Fashanu. It was my house first and the first person to turn up was Fash. I was his bitch at Millwall and I hadn't seen him for years.

'Fash, my old son,' I said, 'how're you doing? Come on in.'

Next to turn up was Carlton Palmer and then Frank.

'All right boys,' I said. 'I'm just going to get changed so you lot make yourselves comfortable.' I then took my pinny with me upstairs and after taking all my clothes off I put it on.

'Is that all you're wearing?' asked the producer.

'That's right,' I said. She went ashen! 'Actually, I'm only joking,' I said.

'Thank God for that,' said the producer.

'Yes,' I said. 'I'll be wearing a pair of cowboy boots as well!'

They tried to persuade me not to but I was adamant.

'Where are we going to put the microphone pack?' asked the sound person.

'Don't look at me,' I said. In the end they made a little pocket on the inside of the pinny and put it in there. The thing is though, because of where it was positioned it made it look like a cock!

Anyway, we carried on regardless and everything went fine until I had to turn around.

'Cut,' said the director. 'Razor, you've got a spotty arse.'

'And?' I said.

'Well, we're going to have to cover them up,' said the director.

'With what?' I asked.

'With makeup!'

Just then this girl appeared with a box of makeup and a big fuck-off brush and before I could say, 'Would you like custard with that madam?' she asked me to bend over. I did as I was told like a good little boy but as she started powdering my arse I started to get a semi-on. *Oh bollocks*, I thought. *What am I going to do now?*

In times such as these I usually try and bring something to mind that would make me go limp so after imagining shaking hands with Susan Boyle and discussing cricket for a few seconds I was as soft as a jelly and ready to go.

Needless to say, I didn't fucking win.

30

My Old Mum

Although my old man's passed away my mum's still very much with us and it would be remiss of me not to use a page or two to pay tribute to the old girl. And tell you about some of the more embarrassing things she's done over the years. After all, if you can't humiliate your old mum, who can you humiliate? I'm obviously only kidding. My mum's got a cracking sense of humour and she'll be tickled pink by this. At least I hope she will.

When I first started getting interested in football she ensured that I ate all the right food. I used to have steak, salad and potatoes most nights. The only reason I mention it is because she used to give my two older brothers Spam and chips, which used to infuriate them.

'Why's he getting steak, Mum?' they used to ask.

'Because he's going to be a famous footballer one day, that's why!'

Was I? She obviously knew something I didn't. Just to add insult to injury, or in this case injury to insult, she'd then give whichever one of them complained about the Spam a clout across the lughole. 'You're lucky to get that, you little bugger!'

Retribution was unthinkable as if Mum found out they'd had a go at me she'd give them both a kick up the arse. It's hard imagining me as a spoilt little git but in my brothers' eyes that was exactly what I was.

'Thanks, Mum,' I'd say, deliberately licking my lips. 'That steak was lovely.'

'GRRRRRRRR!'

Apart from feeding her little soldier, my mum's favourite thing in the world is snooker and her favourite player is Ronnie O'Sullivan. One day I went to a signing session that Ronnie was doing and asked him to sign a couple of things to my mum.

'Could you make them out to Joyce, please Ronnie, and put lots of love?' Just then my mobile went and who was on the other end but Mum. 'It's my mum!' I said to Ronnie. 'I'll tell you what, I'll put her on loud speaker. Hello, Mum, can you hear me?'

'Of course I can fucking hear you, you prick. I'm not fucking deaf!'

I'd forgotten about the language. People assume that my talent for swearing comes from either my brothers or my dad, but it doesn't. It comes from her. I promise you, she makes me sound like Alan fucking Titchmarsh!

'Have you had your breakfast?' she asked.

'Yes, Mum,' I said. 'Here, you'll never guess who I'm sitting next to, Mum. Ronnie O'Sullivan!'

'Whaaaaaaat?' she said. 'Here, he's fucking good that cunt, inne?'

Poor Ronnie looked like he'd shat himself.

'You're on speakerphone, Mum.'

'Am I? Sorry about that darlin',' she said. 'Can Ronnie hear me?'

'Yes, Mum.'

'He is fucking good though, that cunt, inne?'

'Bye, Mum.'

During the coronavirus lockdown I did a Zoom interview on *GMTV* with Piers Morgan, talking about my ticker, and the day before it happened I rang my mum up to tell her.

'Hey, Mum. I'm talking to that Piers Morgan tomorrow. You like him, don't ya?'

'No I fucking don't,' she said. 'If that cunt takes the piss out of you and gives you any lip, I want you to get in your car, drive up there and kick his arse. All right?'

'Yes, Mum. I promise.'

The following day, during the interview, I said to Piers, 'Look, mate, my mum says that if you try and take the piss out of me or give me any lip I have to get in my car, drive up there and kick your arse.'

He said, 'You can't do that, Razor, because of social distancing.

'I told her that,' I said. 'She just told me to wear a mask and gloves while I'm kicking you.' She was being deadly serious!

'Sorry, Mrs Ruddock,' said Piers.

One of the funniest things my mother's ever said happened shortly after the shit hit the fan about Jimmy Savile. 'Not our Jim,' she said. 'What a load of bollocks! Back in the day, when I was up the Ally Pally or at one of the dance halls, if a man put his hand up my skirt and touched my flower it was a compliment!'

I thought, *Yes, get in there! My mum was a slag! Fucking brilliant.*

A week later my brothers came round to her house while I'm there so I said to her, 'Here, Mum. Tell them about the blokes up at the Ally Pally touching your flower.'

Quick as a flash she came over and cracked me right across the back of the head.

'As if I'd say something like that. Do you think I'm a slag or something?'

Then, just for good measure, she gave me another crack. To this day my brothers still think I'm lying and she still denies it.

31

Love & Marriage

The best piece of relationship advice I've ever been given was from my dad. My dad didn't say an awful lot but when he did I always used to listen, and the night before my first wedding he sat me down and said, 'Son, don't get married.'

'Why's that, Dad?'

'Listen,' he said. 'You know Sherlock Holmes? That ain't a man,' he said. 'It's a woman. And do you know why? Because no man's that fucking clever!' At the time I thought, shut up you old git. What a load of rubbish. Now I understand exactly what he was trying to tell me, and what's more, it's true!

Anyway, I ignored his advice and got married, twice. As I said earlier, I've been lucky enough to have been given a second chance in this department and in the interests of keeping this book light-hearted and not getting sued, that's the relationship I'm going to talk about.

After splitting up with my first wife in 2005, I got myself a flat, rubbed me hands together and thought, *Oooh, this is going to be good*. After a few months, though, I found myself staring at the walls. It was anything but good.

Then, completely out of the blue one day, I received a call from what was then known as Combined Services Entertainment asking me if I'd like to go to Iraq and entertain the troops. At first, I was a bit unsure as I couldn't work out how I'd be able to entertain them. I'm fine telling stories in an after-dinner scenario but I'm not a stand-up comedian and I still wasn't confident enough with my belly dancing to perform in front of a crowd.

After being reassured that it would be just pressing the flesh, having a chat and answering questions, I said I'd be delighted, and a few weeks later I arrived at RAF Brize Norton with some spare shorts and some sun cream.

One thing I'd forgotten to ask was who I'd be going out there with and had I actually bothered I would never have ummed and ahhed. The first person to turn up was the Page 3 model, Jo Guest. *Good start*, I thought. The next person to turn up was another model called Leah Newman.

'What do you do then?' I asked.

'I'm a model,' she replied. 'I was a *Playboy* centrefold a while ago.'

To be honest I'd never heard of her, but there was a very good reason for that. '*Playboy*'s a bit upmarket for me, love,' I said, charming her arse off. 'I'm more of a *Razzle* man.'

'Yeah,' she said. 'I can see that.'

Me and Leah ended up getting on like a house on fire and by the time we reached Iraq I was a little bit smitten. Never backward in coming forward I decided to make a move and she told me in no uncertain terms exactly what I could do. It ended with off.

I wasn't deterred. I like a challenge and I had a feeling that if my charm didn't work, I'd be able to wear her down somehow.

When we got to Baghdad we were taken straight to the British Headquarters, which happened to be Saddam Hussein's old gaff. I say gaff, it was actually a palace, and after making our introductions to everyone there, Leah and I went to have a nosey. The first thing we looked for was his eighteen-carat-gold toilet. We'd been told about this beforehand and as soon as we found it I asked Leah to leave the room.

'Why?' she asked.

'Because I want to take a dump in Saddam Hussein's bog.'

She didn't need asking twice.

When I was halfway through I got lonely so I asked Leah if she'd come in and take a photo of me reading a newspaper on this bog and she very kindly obliged. Once I'd washed my hands we went into the bedroom that was adjacent to Saddam's gold toilet and, just for a laugh, I pushed Leah on to the bed. Actually, it wasn't just for a laugh. I wanted to see if she was up for a quick wrestle, if you see what I mean, and after jumping on after her and trying a hold or two it appeared she wasn't. Yet! She was definitely weakening though.

When me and Leah stepped out of the lift into reception there were about a hundred squaddies and as soon as they saw us they all started cheering and gave us a massive round of applause. It turned out there were CCTV cameras everywhere (apart from the bog, thank God) and my failed wrestling match had been broadcast for all to see. Thank God she said no, that's all I can say! Imagine having your own sex tape before you've even had a date.

Just as I suspected, Leah did eventually succumb to my charms (no woman could resist them for long), and when we arrived back in England we started seeing each other. I always describe her as being my best mate and that's no exaggeration. She makes me laugh like nobody else I know and she's also my drinking buddy. I actually call her teaspoon because one teaspoon of whatever and she's pissed. The fact that she's also reasonably attractive is a bonus. She's obviously punching well above her weight but why shouldn't someone average looking like her end up with somebody above average like me? Sometimes dreams can come true, and I saw to it that hers did.

One of the things that used to amuse me when we first started seeing each other was how she dealt with blokes, especially when we were out. They're all over her like flies around shit when we go out (I could probably think of a kinder description) and whenever one propositioned her she'd shout, 'Hey Razor. This bloke wants to take me home.'

'No, mate, I was only joking. I don't really!' Backtrack backtrack backtrack.

People sometimes come up to me and say, 'Look at all those geezers around your wife. Doesn't that bother you?' And I always say, 'Don't be daft. She'll fucking ruin 'em!' She's had it all her life, you see, and if it doesn't bother her, why the hell should it bother me?

One of the other reasons our relationship works so well is because we each have a defined role. She does the washing, the cleaning, the DIY and the gardening (she mows a lovely lawn, my missus), and I do the cooking. Some of you might be thinking, hang on, that's four to one in her favour, you fat lazy shit, but at the end of the day she can't do them properly unless she's had something to eat so my role, if less busy than hers, is no less important.

As I've said, as well as being good around the house she also makes me laugh. More often than not this will happen after she's delivered what I call one of her Leah-isms. For instance, we were driving through Trafalgar Square once and she pointed at Nelson's Column and said, 'Haven't you met him?'

Straightaway I knew what she'd done. 'Wrong Nelson, love,' I said. 'You're thinking about Nelson Mandela.'

'Who's he then, on the column?'

'That's Lord Nelson. He was a sailor.'

'What's he doing up in the air then? He should be in the water.'

'Fuck me, Leah!'

Another time we were driving through Brixton and she suddenly said, 'Hey, I've got a friend who lives here. Right dirty cow she is. She's got a boyfriend for every day of the week. How the hell she manages eight boyfriends I'll never know.'

I didn't even try to correct her and tell her it was six. Silly mare.

This one's a bit random but the night Ronnie Barker died they showed him being interviewed on *Parkinson*.

'Come and watch this, Leah,' I shouted. 'This bloke was an absolute genius.'

After I explained who he was and what had happened to him, she said, 'I suppose they must have recorded this before he died then.'

'Yes, dear, I suppose they must.'

Probably the most embarrassing Leah-ism – so far – was the time she accused Dennis Waterman of being a Tweeny. In her defence she might not have heard me correctly but after I introduced her to Dennis and explained that he used to be in *The Sweeney*, she said, 'Wow! Really? Which one was you then? Our daughter used to love *The Tweenies*.'

Dennis didn't half give me a look.

Another time we were in Tesco and a bloke I know well came up and said hello to us.

'It's you!' she said. 'Your kebabs are the best in Kent.'

'I'm his hairdresser!' he said, pointing at me. This geezer was devastated. He's got about ten salons!

In 2007, a couple of years after we met, Leah gave birth to our first daughter Pebbles and then in 2010 she gave birth to our second, Kizzy. When Pebbles was born I asked Leah if we could call her that and she went mental. 'I'm not naming my daughter after a cartoon character!' she said. By the time Pebbles was born we'd already decided on the name Ivy Grace and everyone who had an interest had been told the same. 'But you know I love *The Flintstones*,' I pleaded.

'I do not give a shit if you love *The Flintstones*,' said Leah defiantly. 'Our daughter is going to be named Ivy Grace Ruddock and that's final.'

The day after Pebbles was born I had to go and register the birth at the local town hall and for some reason I was feeling brave. *Fuck it*, I thought. *I'm going to call her Pebbles Ivy Grace and I don't give a shit what anyone says. Not even Leah!* That was a load of bollocks for a start. Anyway, once I'd done the deed I paid my ten quid or whatever it was, collected the certificate and made myself scarce. When I got outside the town hall I stopped to have a quick look at the birth certificate and when I did so I got the shock of my bloody life. My gaze went straight to the three Christian names, the initials of which quite clearly spelled out P.I.G. I'd just named my daughter P. I. G. Ruddock! Telling Leah what I'd done was the equivalent of coming home naked after a three-day binge with a bird on each arm, a smile on my face and a peacock feather stuck up my arse. I was absolutely bricking it!

'You utter, utter cunt,' she said when I broke the news from the other side of the living room. The only thing that stopped her from killing me was that she'd just had a baby and was knackered, otherwise she'd have had me hanged, drawn and quartered – twice!

'I'm sorry, love,' I said pathetically. 'I was just a bit euphoric, I suppose. It seemed like a good idea.'

She wasn't having any of it. 'I fucking hate you, Razor. You're a selfish prick!'

'Yes, love, anything you say.'

In 2013, so eight years after we met, I finally decided to make an honest woman of Leah. She'd more than proven her worth by giving me two daughters and she also appeared to be aging quite well. Her arse, which was lovely when we met, hadn't hit the back of her knees yet and her boobs were still like new. *Why not?* I thought to myself. *You could do a lot worse!*

After buying a ring I then had to choose somewhere romantic to propose. After much deliberation I decided on a multi-storey car park.

We'd been to do some shopping and while we were on our way out I decided that now was the time.

'What the hell are you doing?' she said when I stopped the car.

After scrambling to find the bloody ring, which was in one of my coat pockets, I found it, opened the car door and ran around to the passenger window where she was sitting. By this time there were about ten cars behind us and every single driver seemed to be blowing their bloody horn. 'Fuck off,' I shouted to them.

After opening Leah's door I got down on one knee, took out the box with the ring in it, opened it up and said, 'Will you marry me?'

She said, 'Of course I will, yer cunt. Now get back in the fucking car before we get lynched!'

Acknowledgements

First of all I'd like to thank James Hogg who not only suggested this little book of mine but also helped me write it. The two of us have had a proper laugh getting it sorted and I even managed to get him wankered the night before an early flight. Get in there! Thanks, mate.

Secondly I'd like to say a big thank you to my literary agent, Tim Bates, and to my publishers, Andreas Campomar and Claire Chesser at Little, Brown. I must admit I have absolutely no idea what literary agents or publishers do day-to-day, but I'm sure it's very interesting. Cheers, boys and girl!

Next up I would like to pay tribute to my three buddies, Tony Clarke, Simon Needham and Lee Harlow Hanning. Over the years their help and advice have been invaluable, as have their numerous kicks up the arse!! Love you to bits, lads xxx

Last but definitely not least I would like to thank my beautiful wife and best mate, Leah. What can I say other than I am one lucky fat fucker! Cheers, darlin' xxx